APPLICATIONS OF PSYCHOLOGY

APPLICATIONS of PSYCHOLOGY

PSYCHOLOGY

Essays to Honor

Walter V. Bingham

Edited by L. L. Thurstone
Professor of Psychology, University of Chicago

Harper & Brothers • *Publishers* • *New York*

Contents

v

Preface

It seems especially appropriate for a volume of psychological essays to be published in honor of Walter V. Bingham, who has earned well-deserved recognition by initiating and promoting psychology as an applied science. It was by his efforts that the first department of applied psychology was organized. That was at Carnegie Institute of Technology in 1915. Many of the current ideas that students now take for granted were then hotly debated. For example, the idea that a clerk could score a test and assign a grade by means of a scoring stencil without himself understanding the examination questions was often considered to be absurd. Many other psychological methods were similarly debated when they were first introduced. Bingham's civilian applications of psychology included many types of problems in the selection of personnel and in psychological services concerned with morale and efficiency of work.

Three or four decades ago psychology was only a college subject. Almost the only thing a psychologist could do was to teach his subject to more college students. In this relatively short time the subject has become a profession in which there are many more practitioners than teachers and scientists. With this rapid expansion in numbers as well as in range of activities, the young profession of psychology is having serious problems about its legitimate functions and about its relations with other professions. Three decades ago none of us could have anticipated the current tremendous pressure from the public for assistance in solving psychological problems. Some of the leaders in our profession are seriously concerned with the proper balance between encouragement of useful applications and the cultivation of caution so that we do not claim more than we can deliver. In a rapidly expanding field like ours, such boundary lines will necessarily be unstable and debatable.

Perhaps the best insurance against extravagant claims for psychological services that we are really not yet qualified to give is to insist that practitioners in training attain a fairly high level of competence in theory, in experimental technique, and in scientific method. A successful training program must steer a course between pressure for trade school methods at one extreme and pressure for the prestige of "pure" science at the other extreme. It is a common and mistaken notion that scientific work suffers in contact with practical problems. On the contrary, scientific work often finds its inspiration in practical affairs. That has been the history of the older sciences and it is being repeated in our young science. A pure scientist can find occasional thrills in adapting his theoretical work to practical ends, and the well-trained practitioner similarly finds satisfaction in occasional excursions into the theoretical aspects of his work. It should not be supposed that this relation is a one-way street. The gains in theoretical and scientific work often have their provocation and motivation in the demand for something practically useful.

In the twenties it was difficult to obtain financial support for psychological research. At the present time we find psychology in a very favorable situation, with general support from industry and government. This is a direct reflection of the fact that psychology has been found useful. In a sense, we must earn our way. To the extent that we succeed in applying psychology to useful ends we shall also have support for theoretical and fundamental research. It is well for us to recognize this debt to applied psychology.

Psychological work in its many applied forms has made possible the generous financial assistance that is now available for psychological research in its theoretical and fundamental aspects. The man we honor here has had an important share in gaining for our subject and profession these advantages, even in those areas where he has not himself been on the firing line of scientific research. Even during the bleak days of the depression, Bingham continued to work on his main theme.

Bingham was a member of the committee that introduced psychological methods in the First World War. In the Second World War he was Chairman of the Committee on Classification of Military Personnel, advisory to the Adjutant General. In August, 1940, he was called to the War Department as Chief Psychologist. He continued to serve in that capacity until after the war.

This collection of essays can be grouped roughly under several rubrics. The series starts with a historical summary that was presented by Dr. Leonard Ferguson at the Penn State meetings of the American Psychological Association in September, 1950. There follows a paper by the writer on the problems of studying creative talent experimentally. The next two essays treat of psychological services in various fields: Professor John Flanagan writes on military applications of psychological principles, and Professor Bruce Moore discusses attitude appraisals in the study of industrial morale. Professor Guilford's paper, which follows, is primarily methodological and theoretical, on the appraisal of interests and temperament.

The major group of these essays is concerned with problems in selection. The first of the group is by Professor F. L. Wells on who should be at Harvard. In that paper we find that not only are students classified as to intellect and personality by their body types but so also are the colleges, including the somatatonic colleges for athletes. Succeeding papers are by Professor Edward K. Strong on the appraisal of vocational interests, Dr. Marion A. Bills on interests in selecting men for the life insurance business, Professor Edwin A. Lee on the selection of teachers, Professor Glen U. Cleeton on clinical methods in personnel selection, and, finally, an appraisal by Professor John M. Stalnaker of a national scholarship program.

Bingham's main contributions have been in organizing and promoting a number of enterprises in applied psychology and in encouraging men to devote themselves to the task of making psychology useful. In this way his influence has been effective in many areas where his name is not immediately apparent.

The diversification within applied psychology is so broad that it is doubtful whether this field has any fundamental unity as to subject matter. The fundamental unity of applied psychology is the recognition that there is a professional obligation, and often intellectual satisfaction, in the problems that call for the adaptation of psychological theory and methods for useful purposes.

Applied psychology is often regarded as work that we do for an organization, an industry, a company, or a branch of the government. In Bingham's work we find a continuous interest in the individual in spite of the fact that most of his work has been for large organizations. For him there does not seem to be any conflict to work for large organizations with his central interest in the individuals who constitute the larger unit. For that we should give him much credit.

This volume of essays was announced at a dinner meeting honoring Walter Bingham at the Penn State meetings in September, 1950. He was approaching his seventieth birthday on October 20. The editor joins with the authors in congratulating Walter Bingham on the attainment of seniority in professional achievement.

L. L. Thurstone

APPLICATIONS OF PSYCHOLOGY

1

A Look Across The
Years 1920 to 1950

Leonard W. Ferguson

Research Section, Field Training Division
Metropolitan Life Insurance Company

When first asked to take this assignment, I demurred on the grounds that I was not a member of the Carnegie group. But the possibility of participating in this program threw such a signal honor in my direction that, being human, I could not easily pass it by, and I have come to the conclusion that I was wrong about not being a member of the Carnegie group. Practically everyone in business and industrial psychology has had his work influenced in one way or another by the Carnegie group. And this makes all of us, in a sense, members of it.

To prove this point, let us take a look at what industrial psychologists are doing today, and let us contrast their activities with those carried on by the group at Carnegie Tech 30 years ago. A recent advertising blurb for that new and vigorous youngster among psychological periodicals, *Personnel Psychology,* states that this field currently covers, among other things, employee selection, employee evaluation, employee and supervisory training, job analysis and standards for classification, employee motivation and morale, and machine design and working conditions. Let us do some exploring and see what kind of research is being carried on in several of these areas. For reasons which will appear, I confine my remarks to the life insurance business.

We shall find it convenient to divide our discussion into two parts. First, that relating to the field sales organization and, second, that relating to home office clerical personnel. Let us begin our discussion with the clerical side of the picture.

How do life insurance companies select their home office clerical employees? In most companies the procedure followed requires that the applicant complete an application blank, submit himself for an interview, give references that we can follow up, take one or more tests, undergo a physical examination, and so on. This procedure is well known, is widely used, and would appear worthy of no special notice. However, I call to your attention the procedure relating to the use of tests. What tests are used, and what functions do they fulfill? I cannot mention all of the tests used in the life insurance business for the simple reason that I do not know them all. But those most widely used are L.O.M.A. Tests 1 to 5. What is the nature of these tests? Who made them? And where did they come from?

Before we answer these questions you may wish to know that the initials L.O.M.A. stand for the Life Office Management Association. This association is a research organization maintained by more than 200 life insurance companies. It does research on problems germane to the running of the home offices of its members. It was established in 1924 and has played an active part in fostering certain of the research which we shall have occasion to describe.

The first of the L.O.M.A. tests which I should like to discuss is

L.O.M.A. Test 1. This is a 15-minute spiral omnibus mental alertness test. It is used by more than 200 companies, and these companies have used over a quarter million copies of the test since it was published in 1936. Its purpose is to predict success in terms of the job level which an employee will attain five to ten years after employment. In the original study, its validity was found to be .60, and this value has been maintained in many follow-up studies.

The second of the L.O.M.A. tests which I mention is L.O.M.A. Test 2. This is a work limit test of mental alertness. It is used by more than 100 companies, and these companies have used more than one hundred thousand copies of the test since 1937. Its purpose, like that of L.O.M.A. Test 1, is to predict success in terms of the job level which an employee will attain five to ten years after employment. Like L.O.M.A. Test 1, its original validity was .60, and this value has also been maintained in follow-up studies.

The remaining L.O.M.A. tests I will just name: L.O.M.A. Test 3T is a typing proficiency test, L.O.M.A. Test 4M is an arithmetic test, and L.O.M.A. Test 5MD is a machine dictation test.

These five tests were developed by the L.O.M.A. Committee on Tests. But where did this committee get its material? We can dispose of Tests 3, 4, and 5 rather hurriedly, as having no antecedents of consequence to our story. L.O.M.A. Test 2, however, was modeled after a test published by the World Book Company and known as *An Examination in Clerical Work*. And this test, as certain members of this audience know, was developed at the Carnegie Institute of Technology.

L.O.M.A. Test 1 was modeled after a famous antecedent, Bureau Test VI, the Bureau of Personnel Research version of the Army Alpha of the First World War.

These comments do not complete my story on these tests. But I should like to leave them for the time being and go on, meanwhile, to a second personnel activity, that of job evaluation. Job evaluation is carried on today by more than 100 life insurance companies. There are four methods in wide use. These are a classification plan, a point plan, a job element plan, and a factor comparison plan. What are these plans? Who made them? And where did they come from?

Let us consider, first, the factor comparison plan. This plan is used by a considerable number of companies in the life insurance business, by many banks, and by many other business and industrial organizations. It stems from the Pennsylvania Company and the Atlantic Refining Company. This plan consists of the evaluation of jobs according to five basic factors: mental requirements, skill, physical effort, responsibility, and working conditions.

The job element evaluation plan consists of a breakdown of clerical work into 149 distinguishable operations. A value has been established for each of these operations and the total point value for a job is determined by a prorating according to the time which the incumbent spends performing each of the elements or operations in his job. The plan was developed by the Clerical Salary Study Committee of the Life Office Management Association.

The point plan was also developed by this same committee, and consists of ten characteristics in terms of which jobs are to be evaluated.

By far the most widely used plan of job evaluation in the life insurance business is that known as the classification plan. It is based upon the principle that clerical work varies in difficulty in terms of the number and kinds of rules by which such work is carried on, and in the number and kinds of decisions which are involved. Classes of jobs are defined and distinguished from each other upon the basis of these principles. This plan has been used longer than any other, having first been introduced into the life insurance business about 1920.

Our next logical question is, "Where did these job evaluation plans originate?" I will defer my answer to this question until I present certain other material.

Let me shift attention to the sales end of the life insurance business and consider, first, the training of agents. Many of the life insurance companies now have extensive and formal programs of sales training. The more progressive of these plans includes class-room instruction and "on-the-job-training" with trainee, trainer, and training supervisor being present during actual sales demonstrations. They also include evaluation forms, charts, and progress guides by means of which the effectiveness of the training given can be determined.

Much of the methodology used in these training programs is patterned after an ambitious program launched by one of the larger life insurance companies in 1931. This program is still in existence and its origins will prove, I believe, of particular interest to this group. But, here again, for the time being I am going to interrupt my story.

Consider, meanwhile, the subject of motivation and morale. We find most companies in the life insurance business much concerned with these two problems. And we also find that one of the pioneer researches in these areas, apart from the famous Western Electric studies, was reported in a series of booklets called *Morale and Agency Management*. This series was published in 1940 and has become the backbone of much individual company effort to motivate and enhance the morale of their sales organizations. The research leading to the publication of these booklets was conducted by an organization predecessor to what is now known as the L.I.A.M.A., the Life Insurance Agency Management Association. We will run into this name repeatedly, so let me point out that it is a research organization, distinct from the Life Office Management Association but, like the L.O.M.A., supported by more than 200 life insurance companies. It conducts research germane to the sales or field management problems of its members.

And now to weave another link in this story, let us consider again the selection of the life insurance agent.

How do life insurance companies select their agents? Again we have the interview, the application blank, various tests, the securing of references, the physical examination, and so on. For our purposes, I should like to single out for discussion the tests and the application blank. The tests most widely used in the life insurance business are the Vocational Interest Test, the Aptitude Index, and L.O.M.A. Tests 1 and 4. The nature and origin of the L.O.M.A. tests we have already discussed. The Vocational Interest Test consists of 400 items and requires a subject to indicate whether he likes, is indifferent to, or dislikes a number of school subjects, jobs, activities, and so on. It was published in its present form in 1938 and in an earlier edition in 1927 by the Stanford University Press. Prior to this, it was known as an Interest Analysis Blank and this latter blank was developed at the Carnegie Institute of Technology.

A weighted application blank is used by many life insurance companies. Some companies use blanks tailored to their own needs, an outstanding example of this being the one developed and used by the Guardian Life Insurance Company. Most life insurance companies, however, use for this purpose what is known as Part I of the Aptitude Index. This test consists of a weighted application blank of 10 items and of a personality test of 96 items. It was first published in 1938, is now used by more than 165 life insurance companies, and these companies have used over one million copies of the test.

The organization which sponsors the Aptitude Index is none other than the Life Insurance Agency Management Association. This organization has been in existence since 1945. It was formed by a merger of the Association of Life Agency Officers and the Life Insurance Sales Research Bureau. The latter of these two organizations, the L.I.S.R.B., was founded in 1922, and it will pay us to look into its origins. In the life insurance business, this organization is commonly considered to be the creature of Mr. Winslow Russell, an Agency Vice President of the Phoenix Mutual Life Insurance Company. He was given considerable assistance in this endeavor, however, by Mr. Oliver Thurmon, a Superintendent of Agencies for the Mutual Benefit Life Insurance Company, by Mr. Charles Hommeyer, an Assistant Superintendent of Agencies for the Union Central Life Insurance Company, and by Mr. Edward A. Woods, a successful Pittsburgh business man and a General Agent for the Equitable Life Assurance Society of America. It was this Mr. Woods, by the way, at whose suggestion the Carnegie Tech Bureau of Salesmanship Research was originally established.

On November 11, 1920, at the fourth annual meeting of the Association of Life Agency Officers, Mr. Hommeyer presented a paper on "The Possibility and Desirability of Central Research in Life Insurance." In the discussion which followed this paper, a motion was made to refer the question of an organization of a bureau of cooperative research to the Committee on Education. The chairman of this committee was Mr. Winslow Russell. In this discussion, Mr. Russell referred to three letters which he had recently received. The first of these was from Dr. Edward L. Thorndike, the second from Dr. Arthur A. Hamerschlag, and the third from Mr. Harold A. Richmond. To each of these men Mr. Russell had directed an inquiry as to their opinions on establishing a cooperative research agency in the sales end of the life insurance business. You will be interested in certain excerpts from their replies. Dr. Thorndike replied, in part, as follows: "I would make the general problem of the central department that of putting the sale of life insurance, as far as may be, on the same basis as the selling of staple commodities, or at least of fire insurance. This involves a study of the whole psychology of habit in respect to purchasing, of the strength of different arguments with different classes, of the establishment of customs, of the references to insurance in schools, books, motion pictures, daily papers and other sources."

Dr. Hamerschlag replied, "In life insurance our work at Carnegie Institute of Technology in the Bureau of Personnel Research and in the school of life insurance salesmanship has brought forcibly to our attention many problems that need cooperative study." These problems, according to Dr. Hamerschlag, were the nature and location of the buying public; the most efficient methods of selling; the selection, training, and supervision of agents; and the relation of the general growth of the life insurance business to commercial and industrial growth.

Mr. Richmond replied, in part, in this way. "The research of such a bureau, as I see it, would extend along three main lines: First, a study of territorial conditions; second, a study of sales personnel; and third, a study of buyers of life insurance." Mr. Richmond proceeded to expand on each of these areas of research and included an estimate of a minimum annual budget for such a research bureau.

Encouraged by these thoughts, several companies pledged their support of a central sales research bureau, and in the succeeding months Mr. Russell was able to solicit and secure definite monetary commitments from a total of thirteen companies.

An interesting fact about Mr. Russell is that during the First World War he was a civilian associate of the Committee on Classification of Personnel, and there, I presume, was much influenced by his contacts with Drs. Thorndike, Strong, Thurstone, Scott and Bingham. Thus, the idea of a central sales research bureau in the life insurance business had its origin in the work being done by the Division of Applied Psychology at Carnegie Tech.

In the organizational stages of this new venture, a young man recently returned from service in the First World War, a product of the Yale School of Law and a member of the recently established Sales Research Department of the Phoenix Mutual Life Insurance Company, asked to be considered for some position of leadership in this new organization. His petition was favorably received. But this young man, Marshall Holcombe, Jr., was not versed in research technique. Therefore, the Phoenix Mutual secured the services of Mr. Harold A. Richmond, a research assistant in the Bureau of

Personnel Research, to come to Hartford to give Holcombe training in research technique, and to aid him in launching the new organization. This process took one year. At the end of this year, Mr. Holcombe arrived in Pittsburgh to launch this new organization under the auspices of, and to all outward appearances, as a part of Carnegie Tech's Division of Applied Psychology. This affiliation lasted from January 2, 1922, to January 2, 1923, when the Life Insurance Sales Research Bureau moved to New York. Later, it moved to Hartford.

It might seem that the connection between the Life Insurance Sales Research Bureau and the Division of Applied Psychology was a short and tenuous one. The temporal overlap may have been of short duration, but the bonds were deep. And we can truthfully say that the Life Insurance Sales Research Bureau and its successor, the Life Insurance Agency Management Association, have carried right down to the year 1950 much of what was started at Carnegie Tech 30 years ago. Let me now put a few clinchers to my argument.

The first project of the Life Insurance Sales Research Bureau was the selection of agents. The Carnegie Tech group had previously been interested in this problem, and had already accumulated a certain amount of information. This information was made available to the Life Insurance Sales Research Bureau, but it was to be analyzed under the supervision of Miss Grace Manson. Miss Manson went at her work with a willing heart and produced two things: her Doctoral dissertation and the first weighted application blank in the life insurance business. To do these things, Miss Manson studied the records furnished by 18 companies for 4021 agents.

Miss Manson found that she could weight several of the items she studied in such a way as to predict production with a validity of .40. The Life Insurance Sales Research Bureau published the resulting blank and it was immediately adopted by several life insurance companies. It was continued in use by these companies until the Life Insurance Sales Research Bureau replaced it with a revised form in 1937.

This revised form was based upon the records of 10,111 agents but it resulted in nothing substantially different from the form developed by Miss Manson in 1923. It did, however, reduce the total number of items and added a few not studied by Miss Manson. In 1938, this revised application form became Part I of the Aptitude Index and, as I indicated before, the Aptitude Index is widely used in the life insurance business.

Part II of the Aptitude Index is a personality test. Work on this project was begun in 1932 and continued until 1938. These dates might lead one to think that Part II of the Aptitude Index was developed independently of any Carnegie influence. But the Life Insurance Sales Research Bureau retained a consultant to do this research and this consultant was a Carnegie student, Arthur W. Kornhauser. It seems that no matter which way we turn we run into some member or into some influence of the Carnegie group. But we still have many more interesting facts to discover.

The second project of the Life Insurance Sales Research Bureau was that of determining market quotas. This project soon led to the publication of a series of monthly sales bulletins. And this monthly series still continues. Assisting Mr. Holcombe in this endeavor was Dr. C. F. (Pete) Hansen, formerly Assistant Professor of Personnel Research at Carnegie Tech. And assisting Dr. Hansen for one summer was Mr. John Byler, a commercial engineering graduate of Carnegie Tech. Soon after their work with the Life Insurance Sales Research Bureau, Messrs. Hansen and Byler became affiliated with the W. T. Grant Company. And there, today, Mr. Byler is Vice President and Treasurer and Dr. Hansen is Director of Research and Vice President of the W. T. Grant Realty Corporation.

It would become a dreary business if I were to continue listing the work of the Life Insurance Sales Research Bureau project by project.

I would crave your indulgence, however, as I point out other members of the Carnegie group who, at one time or another, have been affiliated with the Life Insurance Sales Research Bureau.

The next in chronological order after Hansen and Byler were Drs. Bills and Uhrbrock. Uhrbrock was a Carnegie student and Teaching Fellow (1919–1921). Then he went with Western Union and in 1924 he joined the Life Insurance Sales Research Bureau. He remained here nine months and then went into academic work. In 1930 he joined the Procter and Gamble Company.

Miss Bills was associated with the Life Insurance Sales Research Bureau during the years 1923 and 1924. Prior to that she had been an Associate Director of the Bureau of Personnel Research and later, in 1925, she became affiliated with the Aetna Life Insurance Company. To the Life Insurance Sales Research Bureau, and to the Aetna, Miss Bills took her interests in job classification, testing, merit rating, and the time study of clerical operations. The job classification plan which I mentioned earlier had been developed at Carnegie Tech. While there, Miss Bills installed this plan in several companies. She later installed it in the Aetna Life Insurance Company, and has since assisted in its installation in many other life insurance companies.

In discussing the subject of job evaluation earlier, I referred to the Clerical Salary Study Committee of the Life Office Management Association. I should now like to mention that much of the work done by this committee was based directly upon work which Miss Bills had done, or was, in fact, Miss Bills' own work to start with. The job element evaluation plan, for example, was the result of the joint efforts of Miss Bills and an Aetna colleague, Palmer L. Dickinson. Miss Bills and Mr. Dickinson generously turned their work over for use and release by the L.O.M.A. Clerical Salary Study Committee.

In 1935, Miss Bills was made Chairman of the L.O.M.A. Committee on Tests and it was largely through her influence—although she was assisted by other committee members—that the tests sponsored or developed by this committee were introduced from Carnegie Tech into the life insurance business.

The next member of the Carnegie group to affiliate himself with the Life Insurance Sales Research Bureau was Mr. Herbert G. (or as he is known to his friends, Andy) Kenagy. When Mr. Kenagy left the Bureau of Personnel Research in 1923, he became Manager of the Sales Research Department for the Procter and Gamble Company. He remained with Procter and Gamble for two years and then joined Armour and Company. He remained with Armour's until 1927 and then became Assistant Manager of the Life Insurance Sales Research Bureau. Mr. Kenagy retained this position until 1936, when he became Superintendent of Agencies for the Mutual Benefit Life Insurance Company. In 1946 he assumed his present title of Vice President. While Mr. Kenagy was with the Life Insurance Sales Research Bureau, he assisted in the development or revision of manuals related to selling technique, training, supervision, office management, and the conservation of business. This represented a continuation of his work at the Bureau of Personnel Research where he had assisted in the development of various aids for the selection, training, and supervision of salesmen.

With Mr. Kenagy we exhaust the list of those from the Carnegie Tech group who, at one time or another, have been affiliated with the Life Insurance Sales Research Bureau. The work these people did lives on after them, however, and the Life Insurance Agency Management Association, successor to the Life Insurance Sales Research Bureau, today has on its staff three psychologists. These are S. Rains Wallace, Director of Research, and Donald A. Peterson and Alfred G. Whitney, Research Associates.

Between this third generation and the first generation coming from Carnegie Tech, there was a second generation group consisting of Dr. Rensis Likert, now Director of the Institute for Social Research at the University of Michigan, Dr. Albert K. Kurtz, now

Professor of Psychology at Pennsylvania State College, Dr. John M. Willits, now Associate Professor in the Graduate School of Business, Stanford University, and Dr. Steven Habbe, Staff Psychologist at the National Industrial Conference Board.

Even this, as great as it may seem, does not exhaust the influence of the Carnegie Tech group upon the life insurance business. Consider, for example, Miss Dorothy Goldsmith. Miss Goldsmith was not a member of the Carnegie group, but she attended one of the short courses offered by the Bureau of Personnel Research. As a result of her attendance at this course Miss Goldsmith developed a weighted application blank for use by the Guardian Life Insurance Company in the selection of its agents. This form was adopted by the Guardian Life in 1920, and has been used with only minor revisions ever since. Miss Goldsmith was able to work out a scoring system which, according to her original data, eliminated 54 per cent of the failures and retained 84 per cent of the successes. In addition to developing this weighted application blank, Miss Goldsmith took with her to the Guardian Life, Bureau Test VI and used it until it was superseded by L.O.M.A. Test 1. She also took with her the Interest Analysis Blank and used it until it was superseded by the Vocational Interest Blank.

Consider next, Eugene Benge. Mr. Benge, to my knowledge, has never been in the life insurance business. But he spent a year at Carnegie Tech and became familiar with techniques that he later incorporated into his factor comparison method of job evaluation. He passed this method along to Mr. Edward N. Hay, who has done so much to popularize the factor comparison method, and so we see at last that three of the four job evaluation plans used in the life insurance business stem, in one channel or another, directly from the group at Carnegie Tech.

Another line of influence can be traced through Dr. L. L. Thurstone. Professor Thurstone has never been employed by a life insurance company, but there are three ways in which he has influenced psychological research in the life insurance business. The first of these I have already indicated. L.O.M.A. Test 2 was modeled after an earlier test, *An Examination in Clerical Work*. This test was developed by none other than Dr. Thurstone when he, too, was at Carnegie Tech. The second line of Thurstone's influence is felt through three of his Primary Mental Abilities Tests: N, V, and M, or Number, Verbal, and Memory. In 1940 and 1941 the L.O.M.A. Committee on Tests found that these tests could be used in the placement of home office clerical personnel in different kinds of work, after their initial screening by L.O.M.A. Tests 1 or 2. The Number Test was found to be useful for placement in work requiring posting and calculating operations, the Verbal Test was found to be useful for placement in work involving correspondence or discussion, and the Memory Test was found useful for placement in work of a typing or stenographic character. The respective validities of the N, V, and M Tests for these purposes were found to be .34, .39, and .59. There has been some use of these tests in the life insurance business but not enough, I fear, for Dr. Thurstone to worry himself about what institution of higher learning he will endow with the royalties received thereon. Thurstone's third influence in the life insurance business comes through the adaptation of his method of equal-appearing-intervals to employee evaluation. There are now in existence and in use in the life insurance business over 20 employee evaluation forms of this nature. Of these forms 16 were developed by the L.O.M.A. Clerical Salary Study Committee and the remainder by the Prudential and Metropolitan Life Insurance Companies.

The number of people from Carnegie Tech who have had some influence upon the life insurance business seems almost endless. How about Edward K. Strong? He, too, was at Carnegie Tech, as head of the Bureau of Educational Research. Here he became acquainted with the work of B. V. Moore, Jay Ream, and Max Freyd on interest testing. He took the problem with him to Stanford and there had Karl M. Cowdery determine whether a modified form of the Carnegie Institute of Technology Interest Analysis Blank could be used to discover characteristic differences between different professional groups, whether these differences could be expressed in numerical scores, whether these differences would hold up on new groups of professional practitioners in the occupations concerned, and whether these differences would apply to students preparing for these occupations. Cowdery was successful in each of these endeavors, so Strong proceeded to expand on the work and in 1927 published the Vocational Interest Blank, scorable for 14 occupations. Soon thereafter this blank became known as the Strong Interest Blank and it has retained this popularized title ever since. We cannot follow here all the things Strong has done with his Interest Test, but it will suffice to indicate that it is widely used in the life insurance business. It has had a marked effect upon the caliber of the men hired to be your life insurance sales representatives.

I mentioned Mr. Harold A. Richmond, and stated that he left the Bureau of Personnel Research to go to the Phoenix Mutual Life Insurance Company where one of his tasks was to train Marshall Holcombe in research techniques and to assist Mr. Holcombe in getting the Life Insurance Sales Research Bureau off to a good start. What happened to Richmond after this assignment? He went to the Equitable Life Assurance Society of America where he was joined by another of the Carnegie group, Mr. Thomas M. Stokes. At the Equitable, Mr. Richmond and Mr. Stokes were associated with Vice President John A. Stevenson, formerly Director of the School of Life Insurance Salesmanship at Carnegie Tech. These three members of the Carnegie group worked on the selection, training, and supervision of Equitable agents. This Carnegie contingent later broke up, however. Mr. Stevenson went to the Penn Mutual Life Insurance Company where he later became President. Mr. Richmond left to go into the advertising business and Mr.

Stokes left to become affiliated with the National Life of Vermont. Mr. Stokes remained with the National Life of Vermont until 1926, then he joined the Connecticut Mutual Life Insurance Company and then in 1932 he joined the Metropolitan Life Insurance Company. When he arrived at the Metropolitan, he found that Mr. Richmond had already preceded him by five years. Mr. Richmond is now in the Coordination and Advertising Division where he is General Supervisor of Public Opinion and Advertising Research. Mr. Stokes is Administrative Assistant in the Field Management and Field Training Divisions.

You will recall my saying earlier that one of the ambitious field training programs in the life insurance business was launched in the year 1931. This was the program launched by the Metropolitan under the direction of Mr. Henry North, then Third Vice President. Mr. Stokes had much to do with the early stages of this program and has had much influence upon its content and conduct ever since. He was also instrumental in initiating some test selection research which resulted in a procedure which the Metropolitan used from 1939 to 1945. Among the tests used in this study was the Strong Vocational Interest Test and Bureau Test VI. In 1946, Mr. Stokes assumed his present title of Administrative Assistant and at this time arranged to have several independent research projects brought together and coordinated in what is now known as the Research Section of the Field Training Division.

Three more names, and I have exhausted my list. These are Jay Ream, John Rockwell, and Griffin M. Lovelace. Mr. Lovelace went from Carnegie Tech to the New York Life Insurance Company where, for many years, he was Vice President in charge of their agents' training program. John Rockwell became an instructor in the School of Life Insurance Salesmanship following Mr. Lovelace. Prior to his affiliation with Carnegie Tech, Mr. Rockwell had been employed by Mr. Edward A. Woods and subsequent to his affiliation with Carnegie Tech, he conducted what was known as the Rockwell School of Life Insurance Salesmanship. This school represented, in one sense, a continuation of the work started at Carnegie Tech. Jay Ream left Carnegie Tech to become an Agency Assistant for the Mutual Benefit Life Insurance Company, later became Assistant Superintendent of Agencies and, finally, returned to Pittsburgh as a General Agent for the Mutual Benefit Life Insurance Company.

I have left untouched several other important Carnegie influences. If we had the time we could describe the work done at the Procter and Gamble Company. It has claimed four Carnegie Tech people: Kenagy, Lovett, Lange and Uhrbrock. And these Carnegie Tech people have had in their employ such well-known psychologists as Richardson, Kurtz, Horst, Harold Taylor, and E. B. Royer.

Another line of influence it would be most interesting to trace would be that initiated by Thurstone when he left Carnegie Tech to become Director of Research for the Bureau of Public Personnel Administration. Another would be to follow through on the Research Bureau for Retail Training now located at the University of Pittsburgh. Another would be through the Personnel Research Federation, headed, first, by Beardsley Ruml, another Carnegie Tech man, and later by Dr. Bingham.

To wind up my part of the program, I am reminded of a criticism often directed at the factor analysts. This criticism is to the effect that they find nothing in their factor matrices that they did not put in their correlational matrices to begin with. I would borrow this criticism and apply it to my own generation of business and industrial psychologists. If you, my dear colleagues, had not previously been conscious of it, I hope that you are now aware of the fact that we haven't been taking anything out of the psychological woodpile that was not first put into it by the Carnegie group under the able leadership of Dr. Walter Van Dyke Bingham.

2

Creative Talent*

L. L. Thurstone

Professor of Psychology
The University of Chicago

One of the most important objectives of education is to encourage creative talent, to learn how to find it and how to train it. We need creative talent in all fields of life. Creative talent is in demand in science, the fine arts, industry, and in the professions. In comparison with the social importance of this kind of talent, we have not done much to learn about it.

At the very beginning of this paper we must admit that little is known about creative talent. We have in mind here the intellectual and temperamental traits that characterize people who are able to formulate problems and to find original solutions. Because of the importance of creative talent, it seems worth while to study it experimentally. We shall consider a number of hypotheses about the nature of creative talent and the types of observation and experiment by which it might be investigated.

---

* This paper was read first at The Invitational Conference on Testing Problems at the Hotel Roosevelt, New York, on October 28, 1950.

Let us first try to delimit the problem as far as we can in the present state of knowledge. Perhaps the first thought that comes to mind is to investigate anecdotal material concerning the work of geniuses. If we should focus attention on such studies, we should also select some living geniuses and study them at work. However, to limit investigation to the study of geniuses is probably not a profitable way to proceed.

Let us begin with the working hypothesis that creative talent is qualitatively the same at all levels: in the trades and in the professions, as well as in the rare and extreme forms that we call genius. Most men in the professions and in business do creative thinking; some, of course, more than others. We assume that the thinking which leads to the solution of problems at the professional level is qualitatively the same as that which characterizes the work of geniuses. The difference may be one of power. If this working hypothesis is sound, then we can learn much about creative thinking by studying the working habits of professional men and the conditions that seem to favor the successful solution of problems. Such study might be cooperative. We might study our work habits in relation to successful problem solving. A few hypotheses will be mentioned that we might keep in mind in watching ourselves at work. Such inquiries can lead to clues that may eventually be useful for understanding creative work.

Before eliminating the upper extreme of genius from our inquiry, let us correct a common misunderstanding about creative talent. It is rather common in the field of mental measurement to discuss the distribution of intelligence in terms of a normal curve. At one end of this curve we indicate the low intelligence of those unfortunates who do not have enough mental endowment to get along in competitive society. They are the idiots and the imbeciles. Then, at the upper end of the distribution it is rather common to indicate the range of genius. This is a serious error. If genius represents extremely high gifts for creative thinking, then it is not synonymous with intelligence. To be extremely intelligent is not the same as to be gifted in creative work. This may be taken as a hypothesis.

It is a common observation in the universities that those students who have high intelligence, judged by available criteria, are not necessarily the ones who produce the most original ideas. All of us probably know a few men who are both creative and highly intelligent, but this combination is not the rule. One does not expect to find creative talent in a stupid person, but there may even be some doubt about this statement because creative talent in one field can be associated with a general mental endowment that is mediocre, although there is undoubtedly a positive correlation between creative talent and intelligence, so that geniuses are usually in the upper half of the general intelligence distribution.

The confusion between intelligence and creative talent is common. For example, Quiz Kids are often referred to as geniuses. They would undoubtedly score high in memory functions, including incidental memory and rote memory. But it is doubtful whether they are also fluent in producing original ideas. If this really were the case, then the problem of selecting creative talent would be simple. Other examples are the students who complete their college degrees at an early age. Experience does not indicate that they later produce the ideas that advance our civilization. On the other hand we should expect to find an occasional genius among them.

Those who supervise Doctors' and Masters' dissertations in the universities often have occasion to speculate about this problem. A Doctor's dissertation is, by definition, "a contribution to knowledge." As instructors we work hard to make an occasional contribution to knowledge, but it is difficult to insist that the inexperienced student do likewise. There is good reason why dissertations are often referred to as "pieces" of research—often trivial pieces. Although a tremendous volume of dissertation research is being poured out from the universities every year, it does not offer any solution to the problem of defining creative talent.

It will probably be agreed among experienced teachers that it is not the student with the highest scholarship who produces the most interesting and original ideas in the laboratory. Students who have creative ideas are sometimes erratic and undependable, whereas scholarship might be regarded as representing a certain degree of intellectual docility. Although there seems to be some conflict between scholarship and creative talent, they are probably positively correlated. Several primary factors of memory have been indicated in factorial studies. Incidental memory seems to be independent of the ability to memorize paired associates, and these seem to be different from visual memory as primary factors. Men who excel in producing original ideas should be studied as to the several memory factors.

It might seem plausible to formulate the hypothesis that people who are creative tend to be generous toward ideas. Perhaps they should be characterized as open-minded. Although this hypothesis has some superficial validity, it will probably be found that creative people do not excel in open-mindedness.

By way of further delimiting the problem we might consider the hypothesis that scientific talent and creative talent are not the same. It seems possible for a man to have good scientific talent without being creative. By scientific talent we mean here the ability to handle competently the concepts and methods of a science or profession without the ability to produce new ideas that are commensurate with mastery of subject matter.

Let us turn next to a tentative formulation of differentiating criteria for the creative act. The solution to a problem is usually characterized by a moment of insight in which the significant question is asked and perhaps solved in the same moment. The moment of insight is the critical moment. The thinking that precedes the moment of insight is different from the thinking that follows that moment. We might define the moment of insight as the main characteristic of work that is called creative. It does not necessarily follow that a problem which is so solved is important. A problem that is solved by the creative act of one man may be solved quite casually and routinely by another man with different experience and training. It is the nature of the psychological processes that should determine whether we call the act creative. A creative act may be completely wrong. That is not known until the new idea has been tested.

It is in the nature of creative work that it has some novelty or invention. Whether society considers the idea to be novel has nothing to do with the case. The act is creative if the thinker reaches the solution in a sudden closure which necessarily implies some novelty for him. Problem solving in a moment of insight may involve almost any kind of content. The idea may be artistic, mechanical, or theoretical. The creative idea may be administrative if it solves an organizational problem. It may be a new football play or a clever chess move or a new slogan.

If the creative act is identified by a sudden closure of insight, it is of psychological interest to consider the nature of the thinking that precedes the closure and the thinking that follows it. The thinking that precedes the closure is in the nature of worrying about the problem. In that stage the thinker may have some feeling for the nature of the solution, which is not yet verbalized. He may be able to say that a solution should look like this but not like that. He may be able to say that such and such things are associated with the solution, which is still unknown, and that certain other things seem to him to be irrelevant. The thinker may be haunted by the problem so that he deserves no credit for working at it. Because the solution has not been verbalized, it is difficult for him to discuss it, even though he may have some feeling for the nature of the solution which is to be found. It is as if the partial solution were essentially affective in nature. The solution to a problem is often so embarrassingly simple that it can be explained in a few minutes of a lecture. Instead of pride in the new idea, there might even be some hesitation in admitting the very considerable cost in time and effort. The work that follows the moment of insight may require months or years of drudgery and hard work in testing and developing the new idea.

After an idea has been found relating to the solution of a problem, it can usually be verbalized. At this stage we can begin to apply the various tools that we have been taught: scientific method, experimental designs, and deductive logic. The object is then to test the idea with all the rigorous procedures at our disposal. The method of attack is then quite explicit. Sometimes the solution of a problem consists of a succession of inventions, and it happens not infrequently that the principal contribution in problem solving is in the design of the experimental equipment itself. Our principal concern is not with the later deductive stages in the solution of each problem. We are interested here primarily in the psychological processes that precede each of the sudden closures at which the significant ideas appear. Most of the instruction in scientific method is concerned with the testing of an idea, but this instruction has little to offer in teaching students how to produce ideas. It is this pre-focal stage of the process of problem solving that specially needs investigation.

Although we seem to be unable to teach ourselves and our students how to produce ideas in problem solving, it may be worth while to consider some of the attitudes that favor the production of ideas. In teaching graduate students many of us have had occasion to observe them as well as ourselves in the work of problem solving. We shall consider a few hypotheses concerning the attitudes that seem to favor the production of fruitful ideas and other attitudes that seem to stifle them. Some students have the characteristic that when a strange problem or idea is presented, their first reaction is negative. Some bright students seem to be able to show immediately by clear logical reasoning that the proposed idea is wrong. Sometimes the proof is so convincing that one is tempted to discard further thought about the new proposal. Even when this negative attitude is associated with high intelligence, the result is not likely to be creative. The more promising candidate is one who examines the new and queer proposal. He toys with it and speculates what the implications might be, if they could be demonstrated. Because of the very novelty of the proposal, his impulse is to wish that it could be shown to be true. He asks, in effect, how the world would be different if the proposal could be sustained. This observation leads one to wonder whether those who are inventive and creative should preferably have a certain amount of gullibility.

Some years ago Walter Dill Scott, when he was at Carnegie Institute of Technology, had a test in which he asked the candidate to write some of the implications of a number of strange hypotheses. What would be the practical consequences if we had eyes both in the front and the back of our heads? He might ask the candidate to enumerate some practical consequences if we could swim more easily than we could walk. Scott's purpose was to determine the candidate's fluency of ideas. Some such procedures might be tried in relation to the present problem, but we would probably find that mere fluency of ideas does not adequately represent creative talent. Fluency in seeing implications may be an important characteristic of creative ability, but some forms of fluency may signify intelligence without implying creative talent.

Even if we cannot teach students how to produce ideas, as we can teach them how to test ideas, we might be able to accomplish something by encouraging them, as well as ourselves, to adopt attitudes that favor the production of ideas. Students often have difficulty in selecting dissertation problems. When a student asks us to suggest a dissertation problem, we might encourage him to ask a lot of questions about the field of his scientific interest. I sometimes suggest that he take as an exercise the writing of twenty dissertation proposals in the course of the following week. Sometimes the student is startled by this assignment because he has the attitude that any single idea would be welcome. Our ways of teaching are partly responsible for this type of difficulty.

It seems proper to encourage students to be critical in reading the literature, but the cultivation of such an attitude has disadvantages. When students review a paper or a monograph, they often assume that their task is to tear the paper to pieces and to make the author look foolish if it is possible to do so. Often their appraisal of a paper stops there. If a student reviews the literature with the attitude of tearing it to shreds, the resulting attitude is not wholesome for his own work. It might be better to ask him to review some papers or monographs that he is enthusiastic about. In reviewing a monograph, he would then pay attention to what the author was really trying to do, what he actually did, and how far he succeeded. In criticizing a paper either because of the formulation of the problem or because of experimental and analytical errors, the student could be encouraged to suggest what he would have done with the same problem. In this way the student's work on the literature would be more constructive than if we merely remain satisfied because he has a critical attitude in reading. If courses were always concerned with ideas and what to do with them, with occasional support from the literature, the student would have less difficulty in selecting one of these ideas for his own dissertation.

One of the attitudes that seems to favor the resolution of a problem can be called the method of solving a problem by denying it. One can ask whether the formulated problem, or the halfway solution that may be available, contains some hidden premise that is implied and taken for granted but which is unnecessary for the real goal. One can try to state explicitly everything that has been assumed and which has not previously been made explicit. If any restrictive assumption or premise can be found which we are taking for granted without saying so, and if that premise or restrictive condition can be thrown out, then the solution sometimes appears. For this reason it may be a good policy not to put anything in writing, not even diagrams on scratch paper, until the central problem seems to be solved. The casual sketch may inadvertently commit further thinking to some restrictive error. I asked Professor Barnard in our mathematics department about a problem. He told me that he would think about it. A few days later he came to me with a solution, but he told me that it was trivial and that very likely I had some assumptions that were irrelevant, or else I had not told him about some restrictive conditions that I had taken for granted. The solution that he proposed satisfied the question that I had asked. He was right in his inference that I had not really stated my problem completely.

A hypothesis that should be considered in the experimental study of problem solving is that the moment of insight is often, perhaps always, in relaxed and dispersed attention. Sometimes sudden closure appears after leaving a problem in disgust, or the closure will suddenly intrude when attention is distracted.

In recent years Mrs. Thurstone and I have been working on various scoring problems. The use of tests is markedly affected by the considerable labor of scoring, especially with hand scoring. It is a practical problem to reduce the labor of hand scoring to a minimum. The use of a separate stencil for every page of every test is a complication that should be eliminated if possible. A simple solution appeared as a sudden closure in a familiar but apparently irrelevant percept. In this percept a picket fence across the street was seen through a window screen at our house. There was an optical interference effect somewhat analogous to beating in sound. In this effect the window screen was seen as a universal scoring screen and the picket fence represented a printed half-tone surface. Here the percept was affected by the problem even though the problem was not focal in consciousness at the moment of closure. Attention was dispersed and relaxed. The universal stencil does not need to be fitted to any exact location on the test paper, and the same stencil can be used for all kinds of tests. The answer spaces can be arranged in any desired patterns with the same stencil. The first thought after this closure was naturally that one should have thought of something so simple a long time ago.

I have tried one type of experiment several times with complete failure. On several occasions I have left my work on a problem to walk around the block and to give attention to other things in the hope of inducing a solution by voluntarily dispersed attention. I learned that dispersed attention in problem solving cannot be faked.

Experimental studies should be made to ascertain what kinds of mental work are done best under conditions of muscular tension with concentrated attention, and which kinds of mental work can be done best with dispersed and relaxed attention. Such studies may bear on problem solving. A related and important educational problem is to determine whether the most productive results are obtained by a driving course of instruction where all the student's time is devoted to lesson learning. Another method would be to alternate periods of intense lesson learning with periods in which the student is asked to do problem solving with the same material at a leisurely tempo and without any pressure of speed. Ordinary scholarship examinations would appraise the lesson learning but not the gains in productive abilities with the newly learned material.

We do not ordinarily hear about how professional men get their useful ideas but there is much anecdotal material on how discoveries have been made. Such stories often sound as if discoveries were quite accidental. It is more likely that the investigators had previously identified themselves with a problem in terms of which they interpreted some accidental effect. Scientific discoveries at all levels are probably not so accidental as they look to the casual observer.

When creative work is studied experimentally, serious attention should be given to the inductive factor. This is one of the most interesting of the primary factors that have been identified so far because it has been shown to transcend the nature of the content, including verbal, numerical, and spatial material. One hypothesis that should be considered is that ability in the primary factor for induction may be closely related with problem solving ability. All of the tests that have been designed for the primary factor of induction require the subject to discover the rule or principle in the material that he is working with. It does seem that this ability should be close to, if it is not identical with, the ability for creative work. Although the inductive factor is an important component in intelligence with high saturation in the second order general factor in intelligence, it probably does not alone represent creative talent. If the inductive factor which is heavily saturated in intelligence were the same as creative ability, then there should be a higher correlation between intelligence and creative talent than has actually been found. Problem solving probably represents more than induction. Frequently it consists in reformulating the problem itself and then solving the new problem.

The scientific study of creative work will probably encounter a set of questions more or less analogous to those which marked the scientific study of intelligence. The question that first comes to mind is whether creative talent is some general factor which can operate in many different media, or whether there are different factors of creative intelligence in the different fields. In exploratory studies of creative work it might be well to start with the working hypothesis that creative talent is a general factor, or that it can be treated as such in first approximation. This corresponds more or less to the way in which Spearman started his analytical work on intelligence. We shall then postulate a general factor for creative work, or perhaps a group of factors which express themselves in different media. Whether a creative person becomes a poet or machine designer or composer or physicist would then depend on the various primary abilities of his intelligence.

We should consider the hypothesis that this talent is not confined entirely to the cognitive or intellective domain. It might very well happen that creative work is characterized mainly by the com-

bination of intellective functions with certain temperamental characteristics. If this should be the case, then we should fail if we confine
our efforts entirely to cognitive and intellective functions. The
distinction between cognitive and temperamental traits is not so
clear as used to be believed. They overlap quite definitely. An
example is the first closure factor, which is well indicated by
Gestalt completion tests and by mutilated words tests. The informal
observation has been made that those who are especially fluent in
the first closure factor are temperamentally more alert, quick, and
active, and more quickly responsive than those who rate lower in
the first closure factor. We cannot make this judgment about the
second closure factor, which has other temperamental associates.
Those who excel in the second closure factor seem to be more
frequently deliberate in manner. However, these are only rough
observations which have not yet been checked against actual
performances.

In studying normal functions it is sometimes useful to turn to the
extremes of pathology. In factorial studies of the primary mental
abilities we have found it useful to include in the experimental
groups the most extreme differences in the abilities to be analyzed.
Applying the same principle here, we should profit by gaining
information about the work of geniuses. We should not confine
ourselves to them because they might be very individualistic subjects
that would be hard to manage. By analogy one might expect to
find that ordinary people who have creative talent in some line
would tend to be somewhat individualistic and this probably agrees
with general observation. It may also be found that creative people
are on the whole less outgoing and sociable than the average but
one can think of exceptions to such a hypothesis.

Many years ago I had the privilege of working rather closely with
a man who is certainly known to be a genius, and I am trying to
recall in the present context some of his intellectual and personality
characteristics. Immediately after receiving an engineering degree

at Cornell, I went to work with Thomas Edison as one of his laboratory assistants. I talked with him daily and had good opportunity to observe his work habits. He was a man of many strong convictions and he did not seem to have much admiration for university education. It seems to me that one of his most outstanding characteristics was a tremendous fluency of ideas. For every experimental failure he seemed to produce three more experiments to try. In this sense he appeared tireless. The cot in his office was probably used for lying down to think about his problems as often as it was used for sleep. Thomas Edison had a startling fluency of ideas which spread often far from the immediate problem. He seemed to have an absolutely endless array of stories. Few of them were fit for publication. Especially relevant to our present problem is the great fluency in proposing alternative solutions to a problem. This fluency of ideas should certainly be investigated in this context, but I suspect that there may be different kinds of fluency and that all of them may not be equally relevant to creative work. Another characteristic of Edison was the casual way in which he treated experimental failures. These appeared to be merely part of the day's work and the signal for starting another experiment.

In setting up experimental studies of creative work, it would probably be best to arrange for two groups: one experimental group of men who have demonstrated creative talent to a marked degree and a control group at the same intellectual level but with less productive or inventive talent. In order to make sure that inventive talent is really distinguished from other intellectual traits, the control group should consist of men who have high scholarship and intelligence, who are capable of profound critical appraisal in the same field as the more productive group. Both groups should be comparable in professional prestige.

One naturally considers the availability of graduate students in the universities for studies of creative talent and originality. There are serious limitations to such a proposal. In studying individual differences among graduate students in their ability to produce ideas we must necessarily depend on the judgments of their teachers. To make judgments about students as to their originality is so different from the customary academic judgments about scholarship that there is some question whether we can trust available judgments for this kind of study. We can be sure at the outset that scholarship grades will have only imperfect positive correlation with the desired ratings for originality. It should be a major part of a research program to obtain rather extensive and systematic judgments of the originality of men in various fields and to make close comparisons with the judgments of these men when they were students some years ago. Some illuminating results might be obtained from such a study.

One study might be made with students in musical conservatories where they could be rated on originality and promise in musical composition. Similar studies might be set up in art schools and in schools of architecture. The college curricula in engineering and in medicine are so crowded that there may not be adequate opportunity to judge the originality of students. It would be especially promising to have studies of originality in organizations such as the Bell Telephone laboratories or the Westinghouse and General Electric laboratories. In such organizations there should be good opportunity to differentiate between the originators and the men whose intellects turn more readily to critical and evaluative tasks and administrative duties. Such organizations could not survive and produce if they consisted only of innovators.

In judging men as to originality we must deal with the inevitable conflict between the standards of our day and those of the next generation. In the musical conservatories and in the art schools there might be some erratic young artists of doubtful status at the present time who will be the leaders twenty years from now. We shall certainly make errors in rating young talent. Every field of endeavor has such errors, but it is probably more common in some fields than in others. Work in the physical and biological sciences can be checked more promptly as to its potentialities than original work in the fine arts. Although every field is subject to errors of this kind they are probably less frequent in the natural sciences than in the fine arts.

It should not be necessary to wait for the results of scientific studies on creative talent before taking some action about this problem. Considerable improvement can probably be made in the selection and training of university students by giving serious consideration to creative talent. For a number of years I was chief examiner at the University of Chicago when the undergraduate college was reorganized. Scholarships were awarded annually on the basis of competitive examinations. At one time there was discussion about how the examination should be appraised for the scholarship awards. The simplest procedure was merely to add up the total number of points that the student had earned with equal weighting for the four divisions: the physical and the biological sciences, the humanities, and the social sciences. This naturally gave the advantage to those students who were good lesson learners over a wide range of content. It seemed more plausible that we would select a larger number of future leaders in the various fields by following a different procedure. According to this proposal we should require only a minimum of attainment in the four fields in order to assure communication with the student at the college level. This would be the minimum requirement for eligibility. The applicant should be expected to show marked attainment in some one field. The third requirement should be some evidence that the applicant has produced something new on his own initiative. This might be some production in musical composition or in poetry or in the design and construction of scientific apparatus, some useful invention, an article or publication on some general social issue. It might even be some clever business enterprise that showed initiative and originality. The appraisal of the applicants would, of course, require the pooled efforts of university faculty groups in their respective fields. One of the objections was that these appraisals could not be reduced to machine scoring. The more serious objection was based on educational policy, namely, that we should bet on the student who could demonstrate good scholastic performance over the whole range of the college curriculum. We would probably be selecting a larger proportion of future leaders in the various fields by the policy that emphasizes independent creative effort even though it would require more faculty participation.

There have been various proposals for the selection of university students by centrally controlled examination methods. It would probably be an error to adopt any wholesale method of awarding university scholarships by means of uniform national examinations. It would be better to allow every community to select its quota of scholarship awards by various methods of selection subject to minimum admission standards that would be set by each college. The standards would vary with the communities and with the colleges.

In setting up experimental studies in this field we should certainly include objective tests of temperamental characteristics, as well as tests of the primary factors that seem to be important. These should include the two closure factors, the several space factors, the inductive factor, and several memory factors. Some of the perceptual functions may be differentiating for creative talent. Some characteristics of perseveration may be diagnostic.

One more hypothesis concerning the possible nature of creative talent and a proposed type of experimental study of it will be considered. According to one theory of intelligence,[1] the psychological act originates in the essentially affective and nonverbalized, nonfocal motivations and needs of the individual. The development of the psychological act towards final overt expression consists in

---

[1] THURSTONE, L. L.: *The Nature of Intelligence.* London: Kegan Paul, Trench, Trubner and Co., Ltd.; New York: Harcourt, Brace and Co., Inc., 1924.

successive particularizations. Each of these successive steps can be regarded as a choice point or bifurcation. If the choice point is in focal consciousness, then the decision is subject to rational control and it is fully conscious. If the choice point decision is made unconsciously in the particularization of the act, then the choice is determined instinctively or by intuition, habit, or chance. According to such a theory, a high intelligence is indicated by a choice point that becomes focal in consciousness at an early stage of the act so that a wide range of possible overt expressions is under conscious control. If the act develops under great pressure of motivation or emergency, then it will develop to nearly overt definition before it becomes focal in consciousness and the act is then likely to be impulsive and relatively less intelligent. We might now make an additional interpretation for this theory of intelligence. It seems plausible that there should be individual differences in the ability to be in some kind of rapport with the unconscious stages of the act, even before it becomes focal in consciousness. Imaginative people might have some kind of rapport with their own unconscious thinking before it becomes focally conscious. It might be possible for a person to have the ability for a high degree of abstraction, in that his acts are subject to conscious deliberation at their early stages, and still not be in rapport with his own unconscious thinking. Such a person would be intelligent and even profound but possibly not creative.

This hypothesis could be experimentally investigated. In one type of experiment we might start with a set of several hundred cards with a word on each card. There might be a code of several rules by which a number or a letter is associated with each word. Consider a case where only four digits are used, namely, 1, 2, 3, and 4. Man-made objects might have the even digits 2 or 4. Large objects might have the digits 1 and 2. Whatever the code is, it should refer to the meanings of the words. The subject might be asked to guess a number for each presented word. The first ten or fifteen cards would be presented with their correct digits. The next ten or fifteen cards would be presented without any digit and the subject would be asked to guess for each card. The next set of cards would have the digits given. In this way alternate sets would have the response given for each word and alternate sets would require the subject to guess. No word should ever be repeated unless it is done intentionally to give the subject the impression that he is doing a memory test. It is easy to determine for each experimental set-up the probability of a correct guess. After a while the subject might say that the word "elephant" should perhaps have the number 1, that he does not really know why, and that he is merely guessing. One might tabulate the proportion of correct guesses for the successive groups of cards. When the subject sees the principle he will have all the responses correct, and the experiment is then of no further interest. Our interest would be in the proportion of correct guesses before the moment of insight. This type of study was done as a doctor's dissertation by one of my students.[2] Marked individual differences were found. Some subjects continued at the probability level until suddenly the insight appeared, after which the performance was, of course, perfect. Other subjects showed a marked gain in the number of guesses up to 65 per cent correct before the moment of insight appeared. One hypothesis would be that those who show this gain in the guessing of right answers before insight have more imagination than those who do not show such a gain. It will be recognized that this experiment is similar to current experiments on concept formation. Instead of dealing with a general process of concept formation, we would be interested in individual differences in learning before insight. Experimental work of this sort should be leisurely with ample response time for each guess. The subject's ability to guess right more often than wrong, even

---

[2] BOUTHILET, LORRAINE: *The Measurement of Intuitive Thinking.* Unpublished thesis, The University of Chicago, 1948.

when he feels that he is guessing, is the characteristic of special interest in this problem.

If a research program on problem solving is undertaken by the college board, I fear that a reorientation will be necessary as regards the criterion. The conventional criterion of college scholarship would not be adequate. Furthermore, in the exploratory studies which would be necessary to solve this problem, it is almost certain that the ordinary objective scoring methods will have to be relaxed. It is almost certain that machine scoring must be ruled out. It may eventually be possible to conduct a test for originality and creative talent with tests that can be machine scored, but it would be a serious error to impose any such restriction on research.

The recent presidential address on creative talent by Guilford [3] at the American Psychological Association is a well-considered discussion of the problem. Some of his major considerations are the same as those we have discussed here. Guilford has proposed a rather complete factorial analysis of a large number of tests that represent various hypotheses concerning creative talent. The present paper has attempted only to outline some exploratory studies that might be concurrent with Guilford's more complete and formal program.

In this paper we have considered some working hypotheses that might be helpful in initiating the scientific study of creative talent. First, we may start with the tentative assumption that creative talent is qualitatively the same at all levels of problem solving. The creative act may be characterized by the moment of insight which is often preceded by nonverbalized prefocal thinking. The moment of insight is normally followed by explicit and deductive thinking in testing the new idea. The prefocal thinking before insight should be studied in order to gain understanding about problem solving as a form of thinking. A hypothesis has been considered that the moment of insight can be expected in dispersed

---

[3] GUILFORD, J. P.: "Creativity." *Amer. Psychologist*, 1950, 5, 444–454.

attention more often than in concentrated attention. A research program on creative talent should put the main emphasis on what happens before insight. It is not enough merely to describe the curiosities of the creative product.

We might consider creative talent as determined, in a descriptive way, by the rapport that the actor has with his own preconscious thinking. This hypothesis can be considered as an extension of an earlier theory of intelligence according to which intelligence is defined by the degree of incompleteness of the act at which it can become focal in consciousness. This rapport can be studied experimentally.

The hypothesis should be considered that creative talent is in large part determined by the temperamental characteristics that are associated with intellect. It would probably be an error to look for creative talent exclusively in the cognitive or intellective domain. Even though we know little about creative thinking, we can encourage students as well as ourselves to cultivate those attitudes which favor problem solving, including tolerance for that which is novel. Experimental studies should be on two major problems, namely, to inquire about the nature of the thinking that leads to a moment of insight, and to investigate empirically how to differentiate creative talent by objective and experimental procedures. It is conceivable that we may discover how to select people with creative talent before we learn much about the nature of that kind of talent. Serious consideration might be given to a plan of teaching which alternates between intensive lesson learning and the leisurely application of the new material to original problems. Finally, let me urge a realization of the importance of this problem because the creative talent in our population is our greatest national asset.

3

Application of Psychological Principles and Procedures to the Military Problem

John C. Flanagan
American Institute for Research

Psychologists first began applying the knowledge, principles, and procedures of their profession to military problems at the time of the First World War. In 1917 and 1918 the services of a large proportion of the well known psychologists of that day were made available to the government in connection with the war effort. Prominent in this work were such figures as Walter Dill Scott, Walter V. Bingham, Edward L. Thorndike, Robert M. Yerkes, and Walter R. Miles. The shortness of the period of active cooperation on the part of the United States during this war prevented an adequate period of evaluation and demonstration, with the result that at the end of the war psychologists went back to their academic work and the military authorities did not insist that any program of psychological services be continued in their establishment. A few psychologists maintained reserve commissions or kept up informal personal contact with the military authorities. When the world emergency in 1939 and 1940 necessitated the build-up of the military department in this country, those psychologists who had worked with the services in the First World War were quick to realize the need for a program of psychological research and service in the armed forces. A natural leader in this work who was appointed chairman of the first advisory committee to the army on matters of personnel procedures was Walter Van Dyke Bingham.

During the ten years following the reactivation of psychological research and service work in the armed forces, much progress has been made. This paper will sketch briefly some of the general outcomes of this work and particularly some of the principles and procedures which this experience has shown are of special value in attacking military problems.

GENERAL PRINCIPLES

Several fundamental principles have emerged from the experience of psychologists in working on military problems. A few of the more general of these are outlined below:

1. *It is essential that an over-all program designed to provide maximum assistance to the armed forces in achieving their objectives be prepared.* Much of the early work of psychologists was opportunistic. Military men formulated problems and asked psychologists to assist them in solving them. In many cases these problems were formulated in substantial detail and very little freedom was allowed the psychologists in their choice of type of solution. Frequently the problems were isolated ones concerned with single individuals and it was necessary that the solution fit into a rigid framework already established in the services. Experience has shown that psychologists can be of much more value to the armed forces if they are encour-

aged to participate in the formulation of long-range plans and to assist in the development of integrated systems for achieving some of the goals in the personnel area.

In working in a large organization a psychologist cannot afford to be dogmatic or to insist that this and only this step is appropriate at a particular time. Programs and plans must be modified to fit special situations as they arise and to fit the personalities of those with whom psychologists must work. However, the existence of a comprehensive plan and a long-range program will greatly facilitate the effectiveness of the group in attaining its objectives.

2. *The work of psychologists should be coordinated with that of the operating personnel in the organization.* This cooperation is needed at all stages. It is essential in planning, in conducting, and in interpreting the research studies on which psychologists work. This coordination must include not only discussions with operating personnel but frequent participation in field activities by the psychologists themselves.

3. *Studies should be carried out on a sufficiently large scale to provide definitive results.* In predicting the behavior of personnel from knowledge of their individual characteristics, we are dealing in probabilities and can never be certain of what will happen in any one case, and in addition, all of our measures of personnel necessarily contain large sampling errors. It is therefore necessary that the size of the groups used be very large if conclusive results are to be obtained. In many situations greater efficiency will be obtained by carrying out a single integrated study than by pooling the results from a number of studies which have been separately planned and separately conducted. Recent experience has demonstrated that the most relevant criteria tend to be much attenuated. In the most realistic situations for testing the effectiveness of personnel in military establishments, conditions tend to vary substantially for those tested. The effect of weather, equipment, terrain, and other personnel are such as to provide very unstandardized conditions and

only a tenuous basis for comparing the performance of two individuals. Only with large samples, either of observations or of persons, can the effect of such extraneous factors be reduced to a relatively small size. Unfortunately, in peacetime military operations there are not usually available many persons of whom accurate observations of performance have been made.

4. *The psychologist's work must include the development of practical procedures applying his research findings.* Not only must the procedures be developed and installed but their use must be monitored for a sufficiently long period to establish that they are practically useful in the operating situation. In the process of initial field use it is usual that numerous small changes and revisions are found necessary. The psychologist can only interpret his results accurately and define his problems clearly if he maintains an up-to-date knowledge of the day-to-day problems encountered in the field units.

5. *Periodic review and evaluation of all procedures is essential.* Immediate applications should always be made of new research findings. However, it is to be expected that these will eventually become out-of-date. At the present time weapons, equipment, and the strategy of military operations are all changing so rapidly that unless techniques for evaluating and refining procedures at fairly regular intervals are utilized, even the best procedures can be expected to become out-of-date and relatively ineffective.

6. *The attention of psychologists should be focused on research and development work on military problems and they should be concerned only secondarily with service functions.* Although there is much need for service work in the armed forces it is believed that individuals with professional training in psychology can make their greatest contribution through a carefully planned program of research and development work. Particular attention should be focused on the development of research techniques and of procedures for evaluating the effectiveness of military personnel and military operations.

SELECTION AND CLASSIFICATION

In this chapter, psychological principles relating to specific military problems will be discussed. Although much work has been done by psychologists in other areas it is generally recognized that their greatest contribution to military management has been in connection with the development of effective selection and classification procedures for personnel. During the First World War it was established that tests such as the Army Alpha could reveal individual differences of considerable practical significance for military purposes. This application of the concept of general intelligence to testing personnel in the armed services was one aspect of the development of practical psychological procedures for measuring general intelligence. These tests of intelligence showed high correlation with both amount of formal academic education and rank in academic classes. In 1940, when the military leaders were preparing for the international emergency caused by Hitler's drive for power, one of the first things requested of psychologists by the armed services was a short test of general intelligence.

In the decade preceding the Second World War attention in the field of psychology had been shifting from general intelligence toward a theory of mental organization placing greater emphasis on specific aptitudes. This shift was exemplified by the work of L. L. Thurstone and T. L. Kelley on factor analysis and the publication of a book on aptitudes and aptitude testing by Walter V. Bingham. The work in the services in the Second World War illustrated this changing emphasis and batteries of classification tests were developed in the various services. Thus in the Second World War it was demonstrated that the special aptitudes and characteristics needed for success in particular military jobs could also be measured by appropriate objective tests utilizing either mechanical apparatus or printed test booklets.

The opportunities for careful follow-up of men classified for special types of training and the very large numbers of men tested and sent into training made it possible to carry out research on selection and classification for specific jobs which was much more conclusive than anything previously done. The large numbers also provided an opportunity to study the interrelations of the various types of aptitude and personality tests on much larger samples than had been available for previous research.

The results from administering the air crew classification test battery—consisting of 20 tests and even larger experimental batteries of about 60 tests each—suggested quite strongly that the early hopes of factor analysts that perhaps 8 or 10 or not more than 20 traits would account for all of the important individual differences in the great majority of jobs were doomed to disappointment. On the basis of these studies it appears that at least 50 tests and quite possibly more will be required for an adequate classification battery for military jobs. The most practical solution may well be the development of 8 or 10 overlapping classification batteries each containing 20 or 25 tests. It would be desirable for each of the 50 tests to have no correlation with any of the other tests. However this does not appear feasible at the present time. Perhaps the best example of what our present knowledge allows us to achieve is given by the United States Air Force air crew classification battery. In a sample of about 8000 men only two of approximately two hundred correlations among the 20 tests were as high as .50. Approximately half of the correlations were below .20.

CLASSIFICATION THROUGH JOB ELEMENTS

At the beginning of the Second World War psychologists had little confidence in their ability to predict which classification tests would be related to success in specific jobs. With a few exceptions, such as clerical and mechanical work, it was believed necessary to administer a large battery of classification tests and follow up the individual tests to determine their later success in the activity. By correlational techniques it would then be possible to select a combination of tests which would have predictive value for the specific job. This procedure has many obvious disadvantages. It is slow. The findings become out-of-date rapidly as new equipment is introduced and the job changes. Perhaps the most serious shortcoming is that it is a purely empirical approach and is not aimed at increased knowledge and control.

As a substitute for this procedure the job element approach has been developed. In this procedure elements or components of various jobs are identified and defined. The first step in developing a classification battery for a group of jobs is to identify the critical requirements for each of these jobs in terms of specific job elements or components. The second step is to relate the job elements from one job to those from another by means of logical analysis and empirical test. When a satisfactory set of job elements for a given group of jobs has been identified and defined, hypotheses are developed as to the type of aptitude tests which will predict success in each specific job element.

In doing this it has been found helpful to use detailed rationales. These rationales, in addition to defining the job element, make explicit the hypotheses and inferences of the research worker regarding the psychological nature of the behaviors involved in the job element. A further hypothesis is then made and reported in detail as to the type of test item which would be apt to predict success in the activity defined. As soon as the hypotheses have been confirmed and it is known that a particular aptitude test predicts success in the particular job element, it becomes possible to short-cut the lengthier empirical procedures in the case of a new job with greater confidence in the accuracy of the predictions.

The steps to be followed in setting up classification procedures for a new job are first to determine the critical requirements of the specific job in terms of the job elements. A critical job element is one which has been observed to make the difference between success and failure in the activity in a substantial number of instances. Although differential weighting of the various job elements is probably not feasible at this stage, numerous studies have shown that in most cases no serious harm is done if all of the job elements are weighted equally. Of course in those instances where reliable information seems to be available concerning the frequency and importance of the various components, it is likely that some improvement can be made by assigning weights to each of the components.

The use of job elements of the type described also makes possible the validation of specific tests against specific portions of the criterion. One of the most important aspects of this approach is that the formulation of hypotheses and testing of these hypotheses tend to give the research worker increased knowledge on which to base future predictions.

It should be noted that the only sound way of verifying the predictive efficiency of a specific test is to give it to a large number of individuals before they are assigned to a particular specialty and follow up their success in training and later on the job.

With respect to the classification problem many of those with relatively low aptitude for one job will be found to have relatively high aptitude for another job. This fundamental finding is what makes classification of great importance in the armed forces. Although factors of motivation such as interests, values, and personality and temperament traits do not appear to be as important as aptitudes in determining success in most specialties in the armed forces in wartime, it is clear that in a career service in peacetime job satisfaction and interests play a much more important role. It is important to know that the man on the job has the aptitude for doing it. It is more important to know not only that he *will* do it for the present, but that he will re-enlist to keep on doing it in the future. The importance of this type of job satisfaction has not been adequately realized in the peacetime services.

TRAINING PROCEDURES

Proper selection and classification are fundamental; however there are few jobs for which individuals can qualify, even though carefully selected, without training. The attempts to give personnel on-the-job training, to handle new equipment for which trained personnel were not available both during the war and since, has provided convincing evidence that sound training is essential. Psychologists have much to contribute to the training program. Perhaps the general finding of greatest significance is that military training programs are more frequently inefficient because the individuals are learning the wrong thing than because of the conditions and methods of instruction. The basic problem here, as in the case of selection and classification, is to obtain an accurate definition of the critical requirements for effective performance. On the basis of this definition inferences can be made regarding training requirements and a tentative training course established. It has not been sufficiently widely recognized that training courses of this type also need validation of their content by checking on their results.

Several principles of learning will be cited and illustrations of their applications to military training problems provided. One fundamental principle is that purposive activity on the part of the learner is essential to efficient learning. In learning to shoot a gun or to fly a plane, mere mechanical going through the motions is of little value. There must be a conscious intent to learn. Learning requires activity on the part of the learner. Recent experiments show that some traces of information supplied during sleep remain. However, this cannot be converted to useful activity without effort on the part of the learner. Both listening to lectures and watching demonstrations have their place in an efficient learning program but they should be immediately followed by activity on the part of the learner if they are to be effective.

This leads to the next principle, that instructions should aim at understanding general principles and should insist on the learners applying these to new situations. In military situations conditions are constantly changing. The men need to be trained in such a way that they will have the necessary flexibility to adapt to situations as they find them.

Another important source of knowledge is information regarding learning and forgetting curves. In order for material which is not being used to be remembered, there must have been a substantial amount of over-learning after the level of satisfactory proficiency had been attained. It is probably more efficient in most situations, however, to provide for periods of practice in the skill after the peak of proficiency has been reached. Studies in military situations have indicated that for certain types of skills the peak of proficiency was reached at the end of the training school and after that the skill decreased because of lack of adequate use, until by the time the individual reached a combat unit the proficiency was at an unsatisfactory level. In many situations increased efficiency can be obtained by training the people to satisfactory but not peak proficiency and then switching the task to a slightly different one. This provides a greater flexibility and ability to apply what is learned and avoids unnecessary over-learning of one specific skill. In certain bombing training programs, a longer period on one set of conditions was used than was optimal for most efficient learning.

The final principle is one of the most important and also one of those most frequently neglected in the military training program. This is the principle of knowledge of results. In learning a type of material such as the identification of aircraft, immediate confirmation or correction of the response of the learner is of great importance. In some learning situations such as flying a plane this confirmation or correction is fairly immediate and automatic. Constant firing at targets without knowing whether any hits are scored has been shown to be quite inefficient as a learning situation.

PRINCIPLES OF MEASURING PROFICIENCY

To evaluate training procedures it is essential that we have accurate measures of the proficiency of individuals. To obtain such measures of proficiency it is necessary to sample mastery of the knowledges and skills necessary to perform the job effectively. It is useful to make a distinction between proficiency measures and criterion measures of on-the-job performance. The proficiency measure is what the individual *can do*. His job performance is what he *does do* in the real situation. Proficiency measures have the advantage that they are standard samples carefully devised to require a demonstration of the knowledge and skills critical to the job. Typically they may be called standardized performance tests. Everyone is asked to do the same tasks under the same conditions.

In contrast, in the typical job performance situation the conditions and tasks vary for each individual. Since the tasks are not comparable, it requires a very much larger sample to compare the effectiveness of individuals.

Proficiency tests have the further advantage that they can be given in the training school situation. They provide an immediate check on instruction with respect to the most important knowledges and skills which the training course was designed to provide. Although a satisfactory level of proficiency will not guarantee that the individual will do well on the job it is certainly a necessary condition to his doing well.

One of the most common failures in proficiency measurement relates to the problem of discriminating between various levels of proficiency. Items designed to measure proficiency can be conveniently classified into four fairly distinct levels: facts, generalizations, applications, and significance. *The first level involves the recognition or recall of simple facts and events.* Too often military training courses emphasize in their course examinations this type of factual information to the exclusion of the other and more important types. Knowing the names of parts and pieces of equipment and of types of operations or being able to recite definitions of processes is useful but not adequate for most jobs.

The second level of proficiency involves generalization and the integration of these elements into an ordered system. This level is illustrated by comprehension of various principles, laws, and generalizations and the identification of specific occurrences which illustrate the nature and operation of a given one of them. Thus it ordinarily is more important for an individual to be able to cite an example or illustration of the principle or process rather than merely to identify a group of words which define that principle or process.

The third level of proficiency is designed to include use of a principle, law, or generalization to obtain the solution to a practical problem. In proficiency measures of this type the individual is required to analyze the situation to determine which of the principles he has learned he should use in solving the problem and then to apply these principles to the specific new situation. It is this ability to apply knowledge which provides the necessary flexibility for the man on the job. Confronted with a new situation, he can bring to bear his knowledge of how things operate and predict what would happen if certain specific things were done.

The fourth and highest level of proficiency involves the interpretation of the significance of the various facts and principles for the individual and his organization. This is a question of implications and is primarily a matter of policy determination.

To apply the above levels more directly to a specific job let us consider that of mechanic. At the lowest level the mechanic learns the names of parts, tools, and procedures. Certain skills such as the operation of simple tools and equipment in terms of a set procedure are also included at this lowest level. At the second level is the principle of the gasoline engine, the function of compression, the laws of electricity. The understanding of these principles and laws is quite essential to the work of the mechanic. The third level is the problem level where the mechanic is confronted with a system which is not operating as it should. From available facts it is his job to predict what would happen if certain defects were present and compare these events with the symptoms shown. The fourth level of proficiency is concerned with policy and the significance of the facts and principles, especially for the organization.

In developing proficiency measures to evaluate performance at the various levels a number of technical problems are encountered. Certain principles of psychology which will be of considerable value in developing practical techniques are listed below:

1. *The selection of points for inclusion in the proficiency measure.* In order to keep the proficiency measure to a reasonable length only part of the job may be included for checking. The proficiency tests should be based on those aspects of the job which systematic studies have found to be critical.

2. *The reporting of observations.* In many situations check lists are provided which are to be filled out after the entire period of observation is over. Under these circumstances the accuracy of the checker's report depends to a large extent on how well he remembers what occurred during that period. Many psychological studies have shown that reports of eye witnesses of what happened some time before are entirely untrustworthy. To minimize the blurring and distortions caused by the unreliability of memory, it is proposed that immediate records be made of observations of what is done on the proficiency measures.

3. *Procedures for obtaining objective descriptions of performance.* It is desirable that the proficiency measure be as independent as possible of the individual who reports it and his prejudices. Three procedures have been found to improve the objectivity with which reports are given:

a. The use of pictorial and diagrammatical aids provides precise illustrations so that the checkers may compare the performance with the model shown.

b. Quantitative data such as instrument reading or actual counts or measurements provide a definite basis of comparison on which all reporters can agree.

c. Precise descriptions of actual behavior, such as statements that he did or did not do a particular thing can be checked by other observers and tend to increase agreement.

4. *Obtaining uniform standards.* The experience, proficiency, training, and attitudes of examiners cause them to think in terms of different standards. It is necessary that standards be specified in objective terms if uniform standards for all persons are to be achieved.

5. *Defining the task for the person tested.* In order to obtain comparable measures for different individuals the task which each has set for himself must be the same. It is important that the observer have uniform standards and objective methods for describing performance but it is also important that the person being examined know exactly what points will be covered and how they will be scored. In this way he can know in advance the relative importance attached to such various aspects of his performance as errors and speed. This should greatly increase the objectivity and fairness of the proficiency measures for the person being tested.

6. *The acceptability of the procedures to the examinee.* In many situations it appears to the examinee that the checker is acting on the basis of whim and personal prejudice in evaluating his performance. The examinee is confused because different observers watching the same performance often disagree in their ratings of the individual's skill. If the examinee knows in advance exactly what is to be asked of him and just what the standards are to be, he is much more likely to accept the procedures as fair and reasonable.

At the present time there are not adequate proficiency measures for most military jobs. Development of several measures of this type is one of the most important problems facing those in charge of training military personnel at the present time.

EVALUATING JOB PERFORMANCE

The final criterion for evaluating the effectiveness of selection and training procedures is success on the job. A well-designed proficiency measure will include most of those factors of importance for evaluating the individual's performance. However, some aspects of the job are extremely difficult to reproduce in a standardized situation. For example, it is impossible to reproduce certain types of emergency procedures in proficiency measures without introducing a level of hazard which is not likely to be tolerated in the training situation. Similarly it is difficult to predict whether a person who *can* do the work *will* do it in a real situation.

In many respects evaluating job performance is similar to measuring proficiency in a standard situation. To an even greater extent it is important to provide a systematic definition of the job requirements. The tasks of observing and reporting are similar to those used in proficiency measurement.

The principal difficulty in evaluating job performance arises from the fact that, unlike proficiency measurement where a checker or examiner is supplied to observe each individual and record his performance, in the real situation there is only incidental observation of job performance by a supervisor who has many other duties to perform. Added to this is a serious lack of comparability in the environments in which different individuals perform their jobs.

In this situation also the job element approach seems to be fundamental. By isolating elements of a number of jobs which are comparable and for which standards can be established it is possible to obtain objective records of work performance. Just as in the case of proficiency measures, an over-all evaluation made at the end of the particular period of time is likely to be based on very inadequate data. General impressions are frequently influenced by irrelevant personal factors, the individual's general reputation, or one or two minor incidents which created a strong impression.

A primary function of the supervisor is to improve and develop the individuals under his supervision. To do this the supervisor needs to point out specific things the individual did which were especially effective or ineffective. Merely telling him that he is lazy, dishonest, or sloppy is unlikely to result in any change in his behavior. The use of a Performance Record in which there are systematic observations directed toward the important aspects of the man's job is the only way in which a fair and accurate job performance can be obtained.

To make such a system practical in most job situations a number of procedures are essential. These are listed below:

1. Observations should be directed toward those aspects of behavior which have been shown on the basis of systematic studies of the job to be of substantial importance in performing the job.

2. Only those behaviors on these important aspects of the job or job components should be recorded which fall above or below some specified level of criticalness. Great efficiency can be obtained by recording only those job performances which are outstandingly effective or ineffective.

3. Manuals and forms must be provided so that the behaviors and standards are carefully defined and classified. This simplifies the task of the observer so that his only problem is: (a) to recognize the behavior as referring to one of the described categories, (b) to compare to see that it exceeds the standards for critical behaviors, and (c) record by merely making a check mark.

4. The provision of manuals and forms does much to define the behaviors and to assist the observer in remembering and recognizing incidents which should be recorded. However it is still necessary that critical behaviors be recorded at frequent intervals. In the common lower-level jobs it is found that supervisors forget half the critical incidents they observe in a week.

5. The final procedure is the use of the forms and reference manuals to obtain a brief summary of the individual's performance.

It is believed that the procedures outlined above will enable the supervisor to obtain a great deal of value from his performance record with the expenditure of very little time. Certainly the improvement of performance of the men working for him made possible by his improved quality of supervision should more than repay him for this small expenditure of time. In most situations a much larger expenditure of time than is now given to supervision of subordinates would be a very good investment. Two minutes a day spent in recording the incidents observed the previous day has been found to pay off very substantially in a number of situations.

SUMMARY AND CONCLUSIONS

It is suggested that increased attention to obtaining systematic job definitions in terms of the critical requirements of the activities involved will be of great value in the solution of military problems relating to selection, classification, training, measuring proficiency, and evaluating job performance. The most important principle which has evolved out of the last ten years of experience is an increased emphasis on collecting facts. Though this idea is not new, the careful separation of facts from opinions and the systematic observation of activities for sufficient periods to collect representative sets of facts is different from the practice of ten years ago.

In conclusion it is proposed that there is much to be gained from the more extensive application of the psychological principles and procedures which have been enumerated to the military problems of the types discussed. The application of similar principles to problems of human engineering, equipment design, job design, group organization, and management functions can be expected to be of great value to the military services in the next decade.

4

Use of Attitude Surveys in Personnel Practice

Bruce V. Moore

The Pennsylvania State College

The relatively recent and rapid development of personnel-attitude or employee-opinion surveys marks a new emphasis in labor-management practice. This interest is concerned with human relationships in day-to-day activities, rather than with their formal structure and purposes as seen by top management (13).[1] Surveys of employee attitude can yield results of interest to at least two distinct groups, the social science researchers and the practical personnel men responsible for labor relations. This discussion will not exclude the interest of the first group, but it will be directed more to a summary and evaluation of findings of interest to those concerned with practice in labor-management relations. These will be presented in the form of a series of propositions.

[1] Figures in parentheses represent bibliographical items, to be found at the end of the chapter.

1. *Management needs information from attitude surveys.* There is more recognition of a need on the part of management for a knowledge of how employees think and feel about their jobs and about their relation to supervision and management. The studies in the Hawthorne plant of the Western Electric Company led eventually to the findings that drove home the fact that what the employees thought and how they felt toward their supervisors and management were the important factors affecting their effectiveness on the job (29).

To keep in touch with employees through regular organization channels, freedom for and various media of communications have been receiving increasing emphasis. There is growing recognition, however, that it cannot be taken for granted that all thoughts and feelings significant for management will spontaneously flow from the employees to their supervisors and management, at least not always before they reach a dangerous state. The systematic survey of opinion and attitude is coming to be accepted as one remedy for this (1, 7-9, 20, 25-27, 29, 33-35).

2. *The attitude survey can reveal significant and useful information.* Various techniques, usually the interview or the questionnaire, have been successful. They may not be perfectly valid in revealing the eventual behavior of the employees, but what the employees say, and the fact that they say it, is important. Although the results of surveys are difficult to validate, the research available indicates that when such surveys are adapted to feasible objectives, are carefully planned, the techniques well designed, and questions skillfully prepared, they yield findings that agree with all other evidence. For instance, interviews or questionnaires do not get from workers any reliable information on objective facts, such as the number of fellow workers in the shop or the date when they went on strike, facts which are of no concern to them and which can be obtained from other and more valid sources. Less than seven years after signing an important contract guaranteeing full-time pay,

only 57 per cent could state the date within one year of the correct one, and the average error of incorrect answers was 2.5 years. On the other hand, interviews have yielded information about attitudes, an emotionally toned response, in a labor strike situation that agreed substantially with the secret ballot in the labor union hall (2).

3. *Methods adapted to purpose.* Various methods have been developed for measuring attitudes, and each has its merits when used for the purpose for which it is best adapted. Systematic surveys of employee attitudes by use of direct questions or questionnaires were begun in the early 1920's under the direction of J. David Houser. Kolstead and others (10, 17) have developed the further use in industry of this relatively simple method. Guttman (6) in 1944 described a method for scaling qualitative data from the direct-question type of instrument.

Following Thurstone's (31) development of scales for the measurement of attitudes by psychological principles and of scoring in terms of standard deviation, Uhrbrock (33) was doubtless one of the first, in 1934, to make extensive use of this type of scale in investigating the attitudes of 4430 employees. A simpler method of scale construction which provides for degrees of agreement with a statement was published by Likert (19) in 1932. From the findings of the studies at the Hawthorne plant of the Western Electric Company (29) came the nondirective type interview for revealing attitudes.

The various methods of surveying attitudes have been reviewed and partially evaluated by several writers recently, notably Kornhauser (18), Blankenship (3), Child (4), McNemar (22), McCleary (21), Deri *et al.* (5), Katz (16), and Nixon (26). For the more truly quantitative type of instrument needed in research, the attitude scale is considered more reliable than a single-question type of opinion poll. On the other hand, a quantitative statement of the prevalence of a qualitatively defined attitude, as obtained in a simple questionnaire, is more significant to management and probably more easily understood. In surveying any industrial or business organization, the problems of sampling should be avoided by using the entire population to be considered.

4. *Getting an answer to fit the question.* The really essential feature for the validity of a survey that is most difficult to assure is that the interviewee understands the question so that he answers the same question which the interviewer or writer of the questionnaire thought he asked. This is more difficult than getting the will to cooperate of the interviewee. It is a problem of semantics and includes the old problem of formulation of the question, but it goes further to include both the general background and the immediate setting for the questioning.

During an experiment in interviewing textile workers on strike, the writer found that the word "arbitration" had come to mean in the worker's vocabulary the same as "surrender." To some of these strikers, the question, "Are you in favor of arbitration?" was as though we had said, "Are you in favor of giving in completely to the employers?" for this is what the term signified in their minds before its meaning, as the interviewer intended it, had been made plain (2).

An inaccurate response does not necessarily mean untruthfulness, but rather error in memory of an objective fact or just lack of information. Often persons prefer to risk a wrong answer than say they do not know.

Provision should be made for qualifying the answers to most questions, especially if the question calls for a "yes" or "no," or other brief categorical answer. Often the qualification which the respondent wishes to give reveals his understanding or misunderstanding of the question. Provision for answers to open-end questions, or for remarks, frequently adds supplemental or clarifying information. In a recent survey, there was no question on working conditions, but the provision for free remarks produced a large number of complaints about the poor lighting and ventilation in the offices.

5. *General attitude and specific instance differentiated.* There is often a temptation to generalize from an attitude in a specific situation, or to apply an abstract attitude in predicting behavior in a specific situation, neither of which is warranted. Recently the writer was analyzing and reporting the results of a survey of 1810 salaried nonsupervisory employees in a large industrial organization. One of the questions related to the merit system which had been installed some time previously and which had been described and sold to the employees as a policy of giving raises to those who do good work whether they asked for raises or not. The form of the question asked and the choice of answers were:

In general, which one of the following systems for giving raises do you think is best?
(a) Give raises to those who do good work whether they ask for them or not.
(b) Give raises from time to time for all workers except the worst ones.
(c) Encourage each worker to ask for a raise when he feels he deserves one.

Eighty-eight per cent of the respondents chose the first answer. It would have been an invalid conclusion, however, for the management to believe the employees were satisfied with the functioning of their merit system. This became evident when the same employees answered the following question and only 51 per cent chose the first answer.

What is your company's attitude toward giving raises?
(a) It usually gives raises readily if possible.
(b) It gives raises only if forced to do so.
(c) It is easy for some people to get raises, but hard for others.

Further analysis revealed that the employees believed in the company's general policy on its merit system, but they had little confidence in its application by the supervisors; and the main remedy lay in supervisory training and better communication.

6. *Different variables and segments of the population.* Any survey should provide for analysis of different segments of the population. These subgroups may be under different supervisors or different management policies that produce different employee attitudes. As Katz (16) has indicated, there should be research design to bring out relationships of variables and causal factors.

In a survey of employee attitudes, there were, among 54 questions, the following 2 questions with multiple-choice answers:

I. How do you feel about the company you now work for?
(a) One of the very best
(b) Better than average
(c) Just average
(d) Worse than average
(e) One of the very worst

II. If a good job becomes open, does your company usually fill it by:
(a) Promoting someone who deserves a better job?
(b) Getting someone from outside the company?
(c) Promoting a favorite worker?

TABLE I. FAVORABLE ANSWERS TO QUESTIONS ON ATTITUDE

Division of Company	Question I. Answers (a) and (b)		Question II. Answer (a)	
	Per Cent	Rank	Per Cent	Rank
A	83	1	68	2
B	74	2	48	4
C	73	3	71	1
D	63	4	41	6
E	57	5	46	5
F	47	6	56	3
G	36	7	29	7

The abbreviated data in Table I, reporting the percentage of answers that might be considered favorable to the company personnel management, show clearly that no valid generalization can be made about morale among the employees of the company. In the first place, there are great differences among the divisions of the company under different management heads and supervisors. The question on general opinion of the company reveals a much better picture than the question on promotional practices. Further analysis emphasized that promotional practices were one of the greatest sources of irritation, but this irritation varied greatly under different department heads.

In this same study, attitude varied with age and length of service; and as found by others (16, 17), the new employees and old employees showed less vocational frustration than those on the job from two to five years. Also, attitudes of supervisors tended to be reflected in the attitudes of the workers under them. The interrelationships of these variables are not easily teased out, but they often suggest the spots and causes of poor morale that need attention.

7. *Relationship of certain factors to morale.* There is considerable agreement regarding the significance for morale of many factors. Nixon (26) writes:

"The results obtained in constructing the modified form of psychophysical scale corroborate the findings of Uhrbrock [34] and Bergen [1], namely, that there is sharp and stable agreement regarding the morale significance of many features of work and work environment. This agreement is highly significant. It indicates that many recurring features of work environment have important morale significance in virtually any organization."

Features of the job rated high by employees and associated with high morale were found by Child (4), Jugensen (12), and Mason (20) to be security, advancement, recognition, and high occupational level. Katz (14) found that the variation between two groups of clerical workers lay in the nature of supervision. Good supervisors placed less stress on production as an immediate goal, and more on employee-centered decisions. Poor supervisors spent more time themselves on actual production.

8. *Personnel programs based on surveys.* Personnel policies and practices can be more realistically conceived and made more successful if the thinking and feeling of employees are more objectively known through the findings of attitude surveys. Various writers (7, 20, 27) have reported how employee opinion surveys have revealed remedial situations, misunderstood policies, and training needs. Holdrege (8) reports that 80,000 civil service workers at eight Air Materiel Command bases were given a questionnaire of 146 items on eight aspects of work conditions. When the results were sent to each commanding officer, they were accompanied by suggestions for improving personnel relations.

From a survey of 873 supervisors in industries throughout Pennsylvania in 1946, at a time when the unionization of foremen was proposed, certain conclusions seemed justified. It was evident that better education and understanding in human relations is the primary need for improving the work of supervisors, and this education must include and begin at top management. The supervisors believe they are essentially part of management, but they have not been given the recognition and security that should go with the responsibilities they must assume. The findings not only helped determine the nature of supervisory training, but also resulted in the extension service of the Pennsylvania State College adopting a policy of always surveying the supervisors of an industry before beginning management training there (25). Houseknecht (9) has summarized this point as follows: To formulate a training program currently geared to the needs of a particular work force, it is necessary to spot the problems in which training may be required, decide what part may be solved by training, trace training needs to groups, and determine individual training needs.

9. *Trends revealed by surveys.* Attitude surveys have revealed trends and comparisons of significance for personnel practice. Miller and Remmers (23) report as a result of their studies of industrial empathy that management has moved significantly nearer the position of experts in mental hygiene and industrial relations in its supervisory attitudes; in effect, it has improved definitely in the past few years. The writer in a study published in 1939 (24) reported foremen to be more liberal in their attitudes toward labor than the responses given by students in engineering and in hotel management. The results seemed to indicate that these students headed toward managerial positions were less informed, less realistic, more conservative, and probably more prejudiced, in the sense of having attitudes without basic information, than are foremen and executives actually in business. These students, after entering into the work of the world, need to become oriented more progressively even to catch up with the mores in industry.

SUMMARY

Employee attitude or opinion surveys mark a new era for mutual understanding in labor management. They are needed as a supplement and check on communications from the employees up to top management. Correctly used they yield usefully valid information on what employees are thinking and feeling; these are facts that are meaningful to them and are not forgotten. Survey methods need to be adapted to the purpose, but the simpler methods of measuring the prevalence of a qualitatively defined attitude are more significant to management. In all interview or questionnaire techniques, the most important requirement is to get an answer to fit the question asked. In interpreting responses, a specific instance must be differentiated from a general attitude, and caution used in inferring one from the other. The same care must be used in segregating the data for different segments of the population affected possibly by different variables. As a result of various studies, certain factors emerge as most important to employees, such as security, advancement, and recognition. Personnel programs aided by the findings of employee attitude surveys can be more specific in remedial work and more enlightened in their conception.

REFERENCES

1. BERGEN, HAROLD B.: "Finding Out What Employees Are Thinking." *The Conference Board Management Record.* New York: National Industrial Conference Board, Inc., 1939, *9:* 53–58.
2. BINGHAM, W. V., and MOORE, B. V.: *How To Interview.* New York: Harper & Brothers, 1931.
3. BLANKENSHIP, A. B.: "Methods of Measuring Industrial Morale," in HARTMANN, G. W., and NEWCOMB, T. (Eds.): *Industrial Conflict: A Psychological Interpretation.* New York: Cordon, 1939, 299–312.
4. CHILD, I. L.: "Morale: A Bibliographical Review." *Psychol. Bull.,* 1941, *38:* 393–420.
5. DERI, SUSAN; DINNERSTEIN, DOROTHY; HARDING, JOHN, and PEPITONE, ALBERT D.: "Techniques for the Diagnosis and Measurement of Intergroup Attitudes and Behavior." *Psychol. Bull.,* 1948, *45:* 248–271.
6. GUTTMAN, L.: "A Basis for Scaling Qualitative Data." *American Sociological Review,* 1944, *9:* 139–150.
7. HENLE, DORIS ROSE, "Employee Attitude Surveys: An Analysis." *Personnel Journal,* 1949, *28:* 218–225.
8. HOLDREGE, FRED E., JR. (Air Materiel Command, Dayton, Ohio): "Implementing an Employee Opinion Survey." *Journal of Applied Psychology,* 1949, *33:* 428–435.
9. HOUSEKNECHT, A. H.: "Who Needs Training and Why." *Personnel,* 1950, *26:* 283–293.
10. HULL, R. S., and KOLSTEAD: "Morale on the Job," in WATSON, G.: *Civilian Morale.* New York: Houghton Mifflin, 1942, 349–364.
11. HUTTE, H. A.: "Experiences in Studying Social-Psychological Structures in Industry." *Human Relations,* 1949, *2:* 185–192.
12. JUGENSEN, C. E.: "What Do Job Applicants Want?" *Personnel,* 1949, *25:* 352–355.

13. KATZ, DANIEL: "Morale and Motivation in Industry," in Dennis, W.: *Current Trends in Industrial Psychology*. Pittsburgh: University of Pittsburgh Press, 1949.

14. KATZ, DANIEL: "Employee Groups: What Motivates Them and How They Perform." *Advanced Management*, 1949, *14*: 119–124.

15. KATZ, DANIEL: "The Attitude Survey Approach," in KORNHAUSER, A.: *Psychology of Labor-Management Relations*. Champaign, Illinois: Industrial Relations Research Association, 1949, Publication No. 3.

16. KATZ, DANIEL: "Good and Bad Practices in Attitude Surveys in Industrial Relations." *Industrial Relations Research Association, Proceedings of Second Annual Meeting*, 1949, 212–221.

17. KOLSTEAD, A.: "Employee Attitudes in a Department Store." *Journal of Applied Psychology*, 1938, *22*: 470–479.

18. KORNHAUSER, A. W.: "The Technique of Measuring Employee Attitudes." *Personnel*, 1933, *9*: 89–97.

19. LIKERT, RENSIS: "A Technique for the Measurement of Attitudes." *Archives of Psychology*, 1932, *22*: 1–55.

20. MASON, RALPH L.: "Experience with Employee Opinion Surveys." *Advanced Management*, 1949, *14*: 98–100.

21. McCLANCY, B. F.: "Polling Employee Opinions." *American Management Association Personnel Series*, 1947, *108*: 12–24.

22. McNEMAR, QUINN: "Opinion-Attitude Methodology." *Psychol. Bull.*, 1946, *43*: 289–374.

23. MILLER, FRANK G., and REMMERS, H. H.: "Studies in Industrial Empathy: II. Management's Attitudes Toward Industrial Supervision and Their Estimates of Labor Attitudes." *Personnel Psychology*, 1950, *3*: 33–40.

24. MOORE, B. V.: "Attitudes of Prospective and Actual Executives on Social Issues in Personnel Policies." Chapter 14 in HARTMANN, G. W., and NEWCOMB, T. (Eds.): *Industrial Conflict*. New York: Cordon, 1939.

25. MOORE, B. V., KENNEDY, J. E., and CASTORE, GEORGE F.: *The Work, Training and Status of Supervisors as Reported by Supervisors in Industry*. The Pennsylvania State College, State College, Pa., 1946. Also in *Personnel*, 1947, *23*: 250–255.

26. NIXON, LEWIS M.: "Techniques of Surveying Employee Attitudes." *Public Personnel Review,* 1949, *10:* 23–27.

27. NORTHRUP, M. STARR: "What Is the Future of Employee Opinion Polls?" *Personnel Journal,* 1949, *27:* 341–343.

28. REMMERS, LOIS JANE, and REMMERS, H. H.: "Studies in Industrial Empathy: I. Labor Leaders' Attitudes Toward Industrial Supervision and Their Estimate of Managements' Attitudes." *Personnel Psychology,* 1949, *2:* 427–436.

29. ROETHLISBERGER, F. J., and DICKSON, W. J.: *Management and the Worker.* Cambridge: Harvard University Press, 1939.

30. SEASHORE, R. H., and HEVNER, K.: "A Time Saving Device for the Construction of Attitude Scales." *Journal of Social Psychology,* 1933, *4:* 366–372.

31. THOMSON, KENNETH F.: *A Treatment of Industrial Attitude Data by Means of Factor Analysis.* Ph.D. thesis, Ohio State University, 1948.

32. THURSTONE, L. L., and CHAVE, E. J.: *The Measurement of Attitude.* Chicago: University of Chicago Press, 1929.

33. TIFFIN, JOSEPH: "The Uses and Potentialities of Attitude Surveys in Industrial Relations." *Industrial Relations Research Association, Proceedings of Second Annual Meeting,* 1949, 204–211.

34. UHRBROCK, RICHARD S.: "Attitudes of 4430 Employees." *Journal of Social Psychology,* 1934, *5:* 365–377.

35. WORTHY, JOANE C.: "Discovering and Evaluating Employee Attitudes." *American Management Association Personnel Series,* 1947, No. 113, 13–22.

5

Validation of Measures of
Interest and Temperament

J. P. Guilford

University of Southern California

There seems to be little doubt of the psychologist's growing concern for the validation of the instruments and methods that he uses in professional and scientific practice. This is as it should be. It is necessary for the self-respecting psychologist to satisfy his own scientific conscience with respect to the soundness of his procedures and also to be ready to support his decisions and his claims in response to his public.

Evidences of the current interest in validation are many. The American Psychological Association's Committee on Ethical Standards for Psychology took as its first assignment the problem of the distribution and use of psychological tests. In its proposed code on this subject, validation is an important consideration, directly or by implication (17). In its 1949 annual conference on testing problems, the Educational Testing Service devoted a symposium to the question of what information on validation should be supplied by test authors and publishers (2, 15). An earlier invitational conference (1947) of similar nature, sponsored by the American Council on Education, devoted a symposium to the validation of projective techniques (9, 13, 18). Two recent articles, by Ellis (4) and by Ellis and Conrad (5), investigated and summarized the information in the literature concerning the validity of personality questionnaires in civilian and in military life. In a monograph, Ghiselli attempted a summarizing of the published validation studies for various kinds of tests as used in industry (6).

It is not the purpose of this chapter to review the publications just cited and others like them. Neither will there be any attempt to cover the whole range of validation problems systematically. It is rather the objective to remind the reader and to call to his attention some aspects of validation problems in general that seem to be neglected and, more specifically, to discuss the validation of measurement procedures in the domains of motivation, of interests, and of temperament. Validation in general practice has consisted of various procedures that have grown up in connection with tests of abilities. Although many of these procedures also apply to the validation of measures of traits other than abilities, such measures often require unique approaches because of special problems involved.

CONDITIONS OF WHICH VALIDITY IS A FUNCTION

Validation procedures would be much simpler if tests were used for the same purpose, such as selection; if they were applied to a standard population of uniform properties; if they were required to predict the same kind of criteria; and if tests going by similar names were measures of the same properties of individuals. None of these conditions is satisfied. Nor is the same test always administered under uniform conditions. An index of validity, consequently, is a function of the particular test, administered under a particular set of conditions, administered to a particular population for a particular purpose, with a particular criterion of adjustment as the goal of prediction. Generalization of any validation information beyond the particular combination of conditions always involves some risk. When an index of validity is given in connection with a certain combination of these five conditions, the applicability of that information to decisions concerning the use of the test in any new situation depends upon the degree to which that combination of conditions is fulfilled in the new situation. This is merely a fundamental principle that experimental psychology has taught us.

Variations of each of the five conditions are numerous. There are, for example, a number of tests or test batteries known as clerical-aptitude measures. There is probably much variation among them in the fundamental abilities measured. There are also numerous organizations in which clerical personnel are employed. The kinds of work done by the "clerks" vary from one organization to another and within the same organization. The psychological requirements for success vary correspondingly. For any one kind of clerical work in one organization, there are numerous possible criteria of proficiency.

Let us say that there are 40 specific tasks that a clerk might be called upon to do. The fact that the person is called a "clerk" tells us nothing about which of the 40 tasks he performs or what proportion of his time he devotes to each one. Proficiency in some of the tasks may be readily measured while in others it may not. Which proficiencies are worth measuring toward the making of a criterion, and how should each one be weighted? It would be interesting, if possible, to make an intercorrelation study of all available criterion measures of clerical success.

The kind of criterion for clerical proficiency is, of course, not unrelated to the purpose for which the test is used. In connection with clerical personnel, the test results might be used for selection, for an indication of the kind and amount of training needed, for placement of the clerk within the organization, and for promotion. Placement might involve the adjustment of a worker to his supervisor and to his immediate co-workers as well as assignment to what appears to be an optimal kind of work. The test results might also have use in clinical work with the employee, should the occasion arise.

What has been said here concerning the area known as clerical work applies also to other areas of employment. It seems unreasonable, then, to expect a test author and his publisher to supply, concerning a test, validation information that would be applicable under all the various combinations of conditions that prevail. If there were a number of recognized criteria whose properties are known, within each area of employment and for each type of use of the test and for each type of population to which the employees may belong, then it would be profitable to seek validation information under each set of conditions. The tremendous task of obtaining all such information, however, would make the test unprofitable to the publisher unless the substantial costs of the necessary research could be passed along to the consumer. There is little likelihood that the consumer would tolerate this solution. Under the present circumstances that have been described above, then, it would seem fair to the author and the publisher to relieve them of the responsibility of providing such extensive information as would be needed.

This is not to recommend that the author and publisher should be relieved of *all* responsibility for providing some validation information. The solution, including the division of responsibility between the author and other agents, rests upon a distinction between two kinds of validity: factorial validity and practical validity. The writer has previously pointed out this distinction (7). Factorial validity is a function of the test and of the population to which it is applied. It is usually expressed in terms of correlations of the test scores with the common factors represented among the component variances which make up the total variance of those scores. The population can be described in terms of certain specifications that are related to the factors: age distribution, sex, educational level, and the like. Once this information is established, factorial-validity data are dependable in connection with an application of the test to similar populations. Complementing information would be in the form of the relation of practical criteria to each of the corresponding factors. This information is a function of the population involved and of the kinds of work and the aspects of that work that are regarded as important in the various situations. The writer once urged the social importance of seeking this kind of information (7). With both tests and criteria described in terms of variances in the same common factors for different kinds of populations, the practical validity of any test for use in predicting such criteria could be readily estimated with a fair degree of accuracy. As more is learned about the primary factors, this approach becomes more feasible. Enough is now known about some of the factors to make efforts in this direction worth while.

The responsibility of the test author, under this plan, would include the establishing of factorial validities of his tests for typical populations to whom the tests are applicable and in which they are likely to be used. This, in itself, is a sufficiently large order. But it seems to the writer that it is a reasonable responsibility. The responsibility for describing criteria cannot be so readily placed. The consumer of tests surely has some responsibility. It is he who must take the responsibility of deciding to use or not to use the test. At some future time some endowed agency may undertake the general task of writing factorial specifications for well-defined types of criteria. Until that time, the bulk of the responsibility will fall upon industrial, vocational, school, and clinical psychologists, as it does at present. The author and publisher have some responsibility in seeing to it that information concerning a test is collected from all research sources and made available to test users.

The collection of information on practical validity of tests under present and past conditions leaves much to be desired. The information is scant and often misleading. Ghiselli found, for example, that the validity coefficients for "intelligence" tests covered ranges of about .80 on the correlation scale, even when the job criterion was highly restricted in kind, e.g., to business-machine operation. Ghiselli concluded that "Variation in validity rather than agreement seems to be the rule" (6, p. 264). Margaret Jones made a study of 2100 references on employee selection written between 1906 and 1948 (11). Of these, only 427 were sufficiently complete and explicit to be evaluated at all. Only 8 of the 427 were found to be fully acceptable in the sense of satisfying all the requirements for a "good report." Dr. Jones lists the requirements for a "good report." Although she found that on the whole reports of practical validation are improving, it would apparently be well for investigators to give increased attention to those requirements.

SPECIAL PROBLEMS OF VALIDATION OF MEASURES OF INTERESTS AND TEMPERAMENT

The traditional validation procedures incident to the use of tests for selection apply to many of the measures of interests and temperament. The favored index has been the coefficient of correlation between test scores and criterion measures, though even for tests of abilities, other indications of validity are often profitably used, if not to be preferred. This is particularly true in interpreting validity to the layman, who wants to know something more directly concerned with the usefulness of the test for his purposes. Tests of interests and temperament, because of their greater variety of "scores" and uses, much more often call for departures from the conventional use of the correlation coefficient, especially the Pearson r, as the index of validity. Let us consider next some of the special conditions that, while operative to some extent with tests of abilities, are of greater concern in the validation of tests of interest and temperament.

Almost all the coefficients of validity that have been published were evidently based upon the assumption of rectilinear regressions of criterion measures upon test scores. It is not known how many such coefficients are very low, or even zero, whereas a correlation ratio might have been of substantial size. The possibility of non-linear regressions is probably greater for nonaptitude measures than for aptitude measures. In correlating ratings of supervisory proficiency with the 13 scores of the Guilford-Martin personality inventories, for example, Mackie found that often when the Pearson r was zero or insignificant statistically, the η coefficient for the same data proved to be significant beyond the 1 per cent level of confidence (12). The optimal scores for supervisory prognosis did not always come at one extreme of the ranges but often at some intermediary positions on the trait scales. This fact is more meaningfully conveyed to the test user by showing the proportions of superior-rated supervisors at the various score levels for each trait. Such proportions are often maximal at some intermediate position on a trait continuum.

Linear correlations between temperament measures and job criteria have been typically low, at least generally lower than corresponding correlations for aptitude measures. Ghiselli reports most of the median correlations for temperament measures to be below .40 (6). Against the pilot-training criterion in the Army Air Force, the correlations for temperament measures were typically below .20, although a few were statistically significant (8). Similar findings from other sources have been summarized by Ellis and Conrad (5).

Such findings call for reconsiderations from several points of view. The best attitude to take is not to reject the possibility of useful application of temperament tests but to raise several questions. Granting that the validities are as low as the reported coefficients indicate, and ignoring the question of voluntary biases in scores, would there be value in using such temperament measures in selection of personnel? Would the recognition of possible curved regressions yield evidence of greater validity? Are job-production criteria the most appropriate ones for the validation of temperament measures? Are the effects of temperamental factors weighted sufficiently in the job criteria? The last question pertains both to reliability of criteria and also the differential weighting of different job outcomes. The more obvious evidences of personnel output may not also express some hidden or indirect effects of personnel, effects that could somehow be felt in the profit-and-loss ledger of a department or of the organization as a whole.

Assume for the sake of discussion that the proficiency criteria are adequate and the regressions are linear. Validity coefficients from .20 to .40 would mean that the scores so correlated account for .04 to .16 of the variance of the criterion measures. The largest of these two suggests a respectable contribution, especially since the temperament scores are usually unrelated to any of the aptitude scores. The contribution to prediction would consequently be unique and nonduplicated. The smaller of these two values seems trivial, unless the reliability of the criterion happens to be as low as .60 (which is probably not very atypical), in which case the temperament score would account for as much as 1/15 of what *could* be accounted for. If some .25 of the total variance had already been accounted for by means of aptitude tests, an additional .04 would be difficult to add from *any* source and, as a rule, it is a case of "every little bit helps" from there on. Even if the additional variance accounted for were .02 or .01 and if the cost of additional testing that is responsible for that increment is comparatively trivial, the use of the added score might be justified. Much more attention needs to be given to the cost accounting of using a test. Wasted effort that now goes to measuring the same traits over and over might well go to the measurement of unique qualities. Even though the gain, as indicated by linear correlations against a production criterion, may be slight, the cost of such a substitution could be made up, at least partially, by dropping a duplicating test which would have added nothing to prediction.

It may be that the extent to which any interest or temperament measure can contribute to prediction over a population of workers must necessarily be limited. When there are worker failures clearly attributable to temperamental or motivational defects, those failures may seem to be very important because of their dramatic circumstances. Such failures may be quite rare in the population but by virtue of their striking features when they do occur they may give the impression of importance out of all proportion to statistical reality. The number of traits is very large. If they are all related to vocational success and if they are at all unique the essential contribution of each one would have to be small. Let us assume a criterion of whose variance 80 per cent is predictable by means of test scores. Let us further assume that half of this predictable variance can be accounted for by means of aptitude tests. There remains, then, .40 of the variance potentially predictable by means of nonaptitude test scores. If we assume that there are ten temperament variables, mutually independent, that account for the remaining .40 of the variance, each one would account for only .04 of the total variance on the average, and each one would therefore correlate no more than .20 with the criterion, on the average. If there are 20 such variables accounting equally for the remaining .40 of the variance, each would account for .02 of it and would therefore correlate only about .14 with the criterion. We shall have to contemplate such small predictive values if the number of valid measures is large.

In view of the evidence for curved regressions, it will pay us to consider what this may mean with respect to the utilization of temperament measures. If there is a positive relationship between the measure of a certain temperament variable and a job criterion, we usually think in terms of a high (socially desirable) score as being favorable for job success and a low (socially undesirable) score as representing a handicap. In a case of linear regression, both of these hypotheses will be true and to equal degrees. In a case of curved regression, one of these hypotheses may be true and the other false, or they are unequally effective.

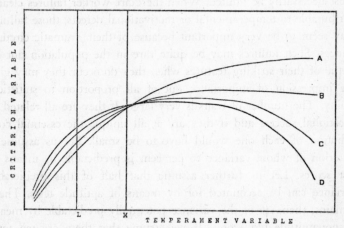

Fig. 1. Hypothetical regressions of criterion measures on temperament measures.

Figure 1 is intended to show what some of the curved regressions may be like. All curves are based on the assumption that the greatest changes in job proficiency come among the lowest scores. In other words, an individual has to be quite low on the trait scale before his job proficiency shows marked effects from this fact. In the upper ranges of the trait scales, the regression might be (1) somewhat positive and almost linear, as in curve *A,* (2) practically horizontal (zero correlation), as in curve *B,* or (3) curved downward (negative correlation), as in *C* and *D.*

Only if employment took a random sampling from the general population with respect to each temperament trait would the entire regression curves of Fig. 1 be realized in practice. There is undoubtedly much prior self-selection in any employment situation. Individuals in the lower region, below L, for example, do not apply for positions. They have gravitated to the ranks of the permanently unemployed, the hospitalized and unhospitalized neurotics and psychotics, or those of low aspirations. If any of the group with scores below L did apply, they would probably be detected either with or without the use of a test. Those with scores between L and M who applied would also tend to be rejected on the basis of the test or perhaps even without it. At any rate, validation study would apply mostly to employees with scores above M. What we would want to know is how well the test would function over the range above L. This is the familiar restriction-of-range problem, which is of some consequence with linear regressions but is of special concern where the regressions are of the form in Fig. 1.

Another possible determiner of the apparently low proportion of criterion variance accounted for by a temperament measure is the phenomenon of compensation. There is recognition of this phenomenon in the effects of abilities when we use the common multiple-regression method of combining scores from different tests to make a single quantitative prediction. It is tacitly assumed that a weak spot with respect to one ability may be compensated for by a strong score in some other ability. The locales, extents, and limitations of such compensatory effects we do not know. They are probably greater in the domain of temperament traits than in that of abilities. It is easy to think of the lack of some specific ability, such as in color-blindness, that would be fatal to success in some job, for there might be no compensating features. On the other hand, many a weak temperament quality may affect very little the productivity of an employee. A weak temperament trait, like the condition of fatigue, is a state that can be covered up in performance, where there are sufficient incentives, such as piece-rate pay or fear of losing a job. The extra compensating effort may make the performance psychologically costly to the employee, to his fellow workers, and to his supervisors, but it tends to prevent the appearance of much correlation between temperament and production. To take another example, an especially skilled workman with high aptitudes has a superior production rate, yet he is almost impossible to get along with. His employer tolerates him in spite of his temperamental weakness.

In the last instances it is taken for granted that the production criterion of the individual is the datum to be predicted. From the larger point of view, there is the legitimate question concerning the psychological, social, and to a certain extent economic costs of that production, and whether these costs should not be assessed against the worker who is responsible for them. The economic costs would be manifest in terms of the production of the unit of which the worker is a part. Total production, or total effectiveness, may suffer through his effects upon other workers, upon the supervisor, and upon public relations. If it becomes evident that poor temperament qualities lead to unfortunate effects not reflected in lowered personal production, the validation of temperament measures should also be done against criteria other than production measures of individuals.

The armed services have generally taken the point of view that it is not good to take into military organizations personnel who are likely to become psychological liabilities. This is partly due to the fact that unfavorable temperament qualities are more effectively related to performance of rigorous military duties than to performance in nonmilitary life. It is partly due to the lack of compensating motivating features in men who did not seek military jobs voluntarily. Under these circumstances, too, there is necessity for reducing the rolls of sick call and of the guard house. Neurotic tendency is therefore regarded as something to be avoided in itself. Criteria have been in the form of clinical judgments which would be strongly correlated with the operational ones of "fit for duty" or "not fit for duty." Screening instruments, even short ones, for the prediction of such criteria were remarkably successful during the Second World War (5, 10, 20). Whether similar criteria would yield comparable validities for the same kind of instruments in industry is open to question. The dividing line between "fit for duty" and "not fit for duty" would be found actually lower on the scale of neuroticism in civilian life than in military life. Even so, this kind of variable, which bases the decision on fitness for duty upon the worker's effects upon his associates and his organization, might be much more suitable than a personal production criterion.

Similar considerations enter into the validation of interest inventories. Interest inventories are more likely to be used for vocational guidance than for vocational selection. Here it seems to be more commonly recognized that those seeking employment of a certain kind, if at all informed, will probably have at least a minimum degree of interest in the kind of work involved. Those actually disliking the kind of work will probably not apply unless forced to do so by other circumstances.

A reasonable hypothesis concerning the regression of job productivity on interest level for that type of work would be a curve something like those of *A* or *B* in Fig. 1. A possible difference might well be an upward acceleration of the regression at the very highest levels of interest. This is suggested by the existence of those rare individuals who say they would "rather work at their jobs than eat." Such an attitude is often accompanied by the development of extraordinary skill and unusual output.

Assuming that the range of disliking on the base line is somewhat comparable with that for liking, the level of self-selection would probably come nearer to *M* than to *L*. The restriction of range among applicants would consequently be greater than for that for temperament traits. Within this range, however, the amount of further restriction between application and validation study is hard to guess. At any rate, the correlation between interest scores and production criteria will probably be low. Except for the possible upturn of regression at the highest interest levels, such correlations may well be lower than those for temperament measures. The relative frequencies of individuals at the extremes where the positive regressions are steepest are low, consequently they would have little to contribute to the correlation coefficient.

While the vocational counselor is concerned about the success of his clients in terms of productivity in jobs, he is also well aware of the fact that interest scores can be very useful in predicting the clients' satisfactions in their chosen work. Few studies have been made with this type of validation of interest measures. Redlener (14) made a study of this kind with both the *Strong Interest Blank for Men* and the *Kuder Preference Record* as instruments of interest measurement. He utilized two criteria: the person's rating of liking for his particular job and his rating for his kind of work. The two criteria are not perfectly correlated. Some men like their line of work but do not like their particular jobs.

Redlener presented data upon 131 men in more than 20 occupations from which correlations could be estimated between Strong and Kuder scores for interests in corresponding areas and the satisfaction ratings. The Strong scores correlated .46 and .45 with job and occupation satisfaction ratings, respectively. The corresponding correlations for Kuder scores were .08 and .57.[1] Such information as this should be a much better basis for the counselor's level of confidence in these instruments than correlations with production criteria would be. As a matter of fact, there is no way of equating production criteria across occupations and jobs, as was possible using satisfaction criteria.

Besides the vocational-guidance use of interest and temperament scores, there are many possible clinical uses. It might be practical for

---

[1] It should be pointed out that the correlation of the Kuder interest scores with other variables is a very questionable procedure because of the strong ipsative properties of those scores as measurements (1). The effect of the ipsative nature of those scores upon correlations such as those reported here is probably not so serious, though the correlation operation is still somewhat dubious.

personnel departments to know the employees better than they do in terms of such scores. There may be much to be gained by the use of such information in forming teams of employees, in adjusting relationships between supervisors and employees, and in dealing with disciplinary problems within an organization. In the evaluation of such procedures, the production of groups, the morale of groups, and the freedom from absenteeism and other undesirable conduct would be reasonable contributors to validation criteria.

The clinical use of measures suggests the inclusion of the projective techniques. It has been generally maintained that the projective techniques, such as the *Rorschach* and the *Thematic Apperception Test,* get at the deeper "layers of personality." It is also often maintained that the results yield a "total-personality picture" that should be treated as a unit in validation. For example, Symonds remarks (18) that the results from a projective test should be treated by analogy to an X-ray picture. Munroe insists (13) that "no device for dealing with many variables at once has yet been developed which is comparable to the trained human mind." The interpreter's report, however, usually comes out with an assessment of the individual in terms of degrees of such qualities as "introversiveness-extratensiveness, anxiety, hostility, creativity, compulsiveness, insecurity, frustration tolerance," and the like. In other words, individuals are, after all, evaluated on trait continua.

There is insufficient space here to discuss fully all the problems involved in the validation of projective techniques. There are many problems, in addition to those mentioned above for other types of personality measures. Some of the chief, unique issues, however, can be mentioned briefly.

First, there is the issue concerning what the projective techniques actually measure. Dependable knowledge of what variables in human personality the projective techniques measure is an urgent matter, in view of the very large amount of research work and clinical practice that is based upon those techniques. Are the trait variables in terms of which the results are now described operationally sound, in the sense that the concepts are dependable (make possible useful predictions) and communicable (one investigator understands another univocally)? This question cannot be settled in terms of feelings of satisfaction of those who use those concepts. Resort will necessarily be made to the more rigorous procedures of intercorrelations of measures, and to that procedure for summarizing intercorrelations, factor analysis. It is too early to say whether the factor-analytical studies now being made of the Rorschach will yield concordant and illuminating results. Thurstone (19) found that scores on the Rorschach had no communality with other of his perceptual-test scores but had some communality among themselves. This would indicate that whatever underlying variables are measured by certain Rorschach scores, they are unique among the factors.

The validation of an instrument like the Rorschach for selection purposes (also for assessing individuals on single trait scales) invites several approaches. In spite of the objections of the users of projective methods, some investigators have attempted to study the validity of single, obtained scores. This is the most objective approach; the approach of the empiricist. The argument is that if the single scores contain information on which an interpreter can depend in making predictions of criteria, the contribution of each score to the prediction should be evident in terms of non-zero correlations against criteria, industrial or clinical.

The clinician's answer to this is that the same score on one of the test variables may mean something very different in two different individuals, depending upon concomitant scores on other variables. Apparently, the meaningful contribution of any single score is so random over the population or so well balanced in its bipolar meaning that zero correlations are to be expected. Two instances of such insignificant correlations can be cited, one from an industrial (military) situation and the other from a clinical situation. The former was the attempt by aviation psychologists to predict pilot-training success from single scores on both the Rorschach and the TAT during World War II (8, Ch. 24). The latter was a serious study to determine whether the traditionally accepted signs of anxiety derived from the Rorschach would correlate with anxiety as diagnosed independently by either psychiatrists, psychologists, or social workers (16).

The clinician prefers to make "global" predictions, using his own summarizing abilities in the inspection of the projective record. The validation of such judgments is a validation of the instrument plus the interpreter. Validation of the instrument could presumably be made by using a consensus of several interpreters or the mean validity index of several interpreters' judgments. This method, however, is not immaculate so far as the instrument is concerned, unless the only information the interpreters have is in the form of protocols. Some will say that this is not fair to the instrument, since the usual application is one in which the interpreter is also the administrator of the instrument. To meet this difficulty, Shaffer has recommended that we validate the interpreter with and without the use of the instrument (15). The use of several interpreters would still be needed to give a conclusion less dependent upon properties of individual judges.

Examples of the validation of subjective summarizations of projective data can be cited from the same two sources mentioned above. The Air Force clinical predictions of pilot-training success based on either the Rorschach or the TAT results correlated insignificantly with the criterion (8, Ch. 24). Furthermore, the two predictions correlated insignificantly with each other. In the study of anxiety, seven interpreters were given 20 protocols and were told that 10 came from individuals diagnosed as having considerable anxiety (some of the most severe among 115 patients) and 10 came from those showing the least anxiety. While there was much agreement among interpreters as to the sorting of the cases into the two categories, no interpreter succeeded in having a score of correct placements that was significantly different from chance.

There are in the literature some reports of subjective predictions that correlate substantially with practical criteria, for example, the prediction of academic success in college by Munroe (13). Such studies should be multiplied, with several interpreters involved, before many of the practices with projective techniques can be said to have anything but "faith" validity. If there are stable, meaningful combinations of responses or scores that can be used for predictive purposes, there are empirical methods for establishing the validity of those combinations. Cronbach has made a promising start toward a procedure for dealing objectively with such patterns (3). Patterns, also, can be subjected to validation procedures.

The assertion that projective techniques get at the deeper levels of personality needs some attention in connection with validation. Would this mean that projective methods have greater potentiality for predicting vocational adjustment?

Two or three studies, especially with the use of the TAT, have shown low correlations between the kind of personality revealed and the kind as shown by the conduct of individuals. In one such investigation by Symonds (18), further study did show that the TAT results predicted the phantasy life of the children involved, but in many individuals phantasy life and actual behavior were almost opposite in character. There was better agreement between phantasy life and overt behavior among the well-adjusted children than among the poorly-adjusted. Taking well-adjusted and poorly-adjusted together in a sample, the prediction of overt behavior from TAT results was poor. Validation results based upon the entire sample would have led to the conclusion that TAT results do not predict overt behavior. Results for the poorly-adjusted alone would have led to a conclusion of negative correlation between TAT findings and overt behavior.

There is something of a psychological dilemma in this situation. On the one hand, there is the assumption that the deeper levels of personality do have a significant relation to the overt conduct of the individual. This is the chief excuse for the approach to the understanding of behavior problems by way of those levels. On the other hand, if the relationship is sufficiently strong, one should be able to assess the conditions in the deeper levels by observation of overt behavior; in other words, by means of more superficial (less projective) methods. It has been found that prediction of future behavior can be made with greater confidence on the basis of more superficial methods (9). These considerations, taken together, leave us with some doubt about the importance of seeking information concerning the deeper levels for the prediction of vocational adjustment.

The dilemma cannot be solved until we know more about the psychological variables indicated by both the superficial and the projective approaches and about their agreements and their disagreements. The reasons for disagreements will probably be found in terms of the phenomena of control and compensation. It may be well worth while to know about both the manifest and the latent traits of each individual. Where there is notable disagreement one might be forewarned of inconsistencies in overt behavior and of apparently sudden reversals of character. Clinical attention to individuals showing such disagreements might well prevent the scrupulously honest person suddenly becoming guilty of embezzlement and the sunny and cheerful person suddenly going on a homicidal binge. Such cases are rare, but they are the kind that help to strengthen the conviction that temperament is important in the employment situation and they are the kind that projective techniques should be best adapted to predicting.

REFERENCES

1. CATTELL, R. B.: "Psychological measurement: ipsative, normative, and interactive." *Psychol. Rev.*, 1944, *51*: 292–303.
2. CONRAD, H.: "Aptitude and intelligence tests," in *Proceedings, 1949*

Invitational Conference on Testing Problems. Princeton, N. J.: Educational Testing Service, 1940.

3. Cronbach, L. J.: "Pattern tabulation: A statistical method for analysis of limited patterns of scores, with particular reference to the Rorschach test." *Educ. & Psychol. Meas.,* 1949, *9:* 149–171.

4. Ellis, A. J.: "The validity of personality questionnaires." *Psychol. Bull.,* 1946, *43:* 385–440.

5. Ellis, A. J., and Conrad, H. S.: "The validity of personality inventories in military practice." *Psychol. Bull.,* 1948, *45:* 385–420.

6. Ghiselli, E. E.: "The validity of commonly employed occupational tests." *The University of California Publications in Psychology.* 1949, *5:* 253–288.

7. Guilford, J. P.: "New standards for test evaluation." *Educ. & Psychol. Meas.* 1946, *6:* 427–438.

8. Guilford, J. P. (Ed.): *Army Air Forces Aviation Psychology Research Program Reports. No. 5, Printed Classification Tests.* Washington, D. C.: Government Printing Office, 1947.

9. Hanfmann, E.: "Projective techniques in the assessment program of the office of strategic services," in *Exploring Individual Differences.* Washington, D. C.: American Council on Education, 1947.

10. Hunt, W. A., and Stevenson, I.: "Psychological testing in military clinical psychology." *Psychol. Rev.* 1946, *53:* 107–115.

11. Jones, M. H.: "The adequacy of employee selection reports." *J. Appl. Psychol.,* 1950, *34:* 219–224.

12. Mackie, R. R.: *Norms and Validities of Sixteen Test Variables for Predicting Success of Foremen.* A Master's thesis, University of Southern California Library, 1948.

13. Munroe, R. L.: "Academic success and personal adjustment in college," in *Exploring Individual Differences.* Washington, D. C.: American Council on Education, 1947.

14. Redlener, J.: *A Comparative Study of the Efficiency of the Kuder Preference Record and the Strong Vocational Interest Blank in the Prediction of Job Satisfaction.* A Master's thesis, University of Southern California Library, 1948.

15. Shaffer, L. F.: "Personality tests," in *Proceedings, 1949 Invitational*

Conference on Testing Problems. Princeton, N. J.: Educational Testing Service, 1949.

16. STEWART, B. A.: *A Study of the Relationship between Clinical Manifestations of Neurotic Anxiety and Rorschach Test Performance.* A Doctor's dissertation, University of Southern California Library, 1950.

17. SUPER, D. E., *et al.*: "Ethical standards for the distribution of psychological tests and diagnostic aids." *Amer. Psychologist,* 1940, *4:* 495–501.

18. Symonds, P. M.: "Survey of projective techniques," in *Exploring Individual Differences.* Washington, D. C.: American Council on Education, 1947.

19. THURSTONE, L. L.: *A Factorial Study of Perception.* Chicago: University of Chicago Press, 1944.

20. ZUBIN, J.: "Recent advances in screening the emotionally maladjusted." *J. Clin. Psychol.,* 1948, *4:* 56–63.

6

Should This Student
Be At Harvard?

F. L. Wells

Study of Adult Development (Grant Study)
Department of Hygiene, Harvard University

In about one fifth of the cases referred to the writer's office, the referral problem concerns the basic adaptability of the student to the local academic environment. Two factors are involved: intellectual endowment, and temperamental fitness to apply it in this setting. Some attempt is made to classify the material according as one or the other factor is clearly uppermost. More precise delimitations may be gained by noting other categories into which the general body of referral material may be classified. In the most numerous group, comprising perhaps a third of all referrals, the central problem is not academic, but concerns a usually minor and incidental psychiatric symptom-complex. The only other large grouping is concerned with career plan, and includes about a fourth of the referrals. These figures are slightly low, because scattering cases of special technical interest, e.g., projective test interpretation, may be classified accordingly, but they are substantially representative. The most distinctive remaining category, from a psychometric standpoint, are the bi- or multilinguals, with the special problems that they present in the evaluation of intellectual functions. Only the 20 per cent of referrals noted at the outset are concerned in this presentation.

Among those who were enrolled as students, whether as graduates or undergraduates, this problem of basic adaptability seems to arise (overtly) more often on intellectual than on temperamental grounds, some two or three times as often. Among those not enrolled, on the other hand, a similar preponderance of temperamental factors is indicated. The reason for this is probably administrative. If a previous separation had been on intellectual grounds (academic performance) essentially, the question of readmission might well be decided by admitting authorities without reference to the Hygiene Department. But if the separation seemed to have involved temperamental factors, approval by the Hygiene Department from a psychiatric standpoint would probably be requested, with consequent referral to the present office.

The title question is purposely so framed as to include both those enrolled and not enrolled at the time of referral. Of the latter, many have been, as above, separated from the University after an original admission, and now seek readmission. The question has claim to consideration from the standpoint of both the student (is this a good place for him?) and the institution (is the admission or retention of this man in proper accord with its educational responsibilities?). The referring agent, usually a psychiatrist of the Department of Hygiene, and this writer have the aim and function of balancing these claims clinically, for the individual case, and immediate concern is with illustrations of these problems.

Prominently associated with student adjustment difficulties is parental pressure to attend some particular institution, e.g., Harvard, upon students whose motivation is lacking if not negative. Unfortunately the basis for a balanced view of this situation is also lacking. Only those students who have not adjusted well to such direction would come to notice of this sort. It is not impossible that for every such case there is another for whom the parental pressure was well advised, and who in after years is grateful for the direction imposed. The Grant Study by definition excluded difficulties of Hygiene Department referral level. But it contains cases where the student came here under parental pressure, against inclination, later doing well in college, where parental pressure seemed thoroughly appropriate. There is a particular instance in which, as above, the student went through college "somewhat against his will. His father was very proud of him for being in Harvard and urged him on, but the boy felt . . . that he was not a student . . . did not have a real interest. . . . Later he grew to value his college education. . . . He wanted his own son to come to Harvard and get all A's."

The role of parental pressure must thus be judged by the wisdom of the source and the maturity of the prospective student. Often the pressure has less than no rational basis, and institutions are subject to such applications in proportion to their prestige. From an actuarial standpoint, a large institution can accept certain risks of this sort with its eyes open. Clinically it is less justifiable to incur them, when so much of individual success and happiness is at stake.

From existing distinctions between higher educational institutions, one can postulate the human qualities to which a given college has the most to offer. The type of institution which Harvard represents makes its principal appeal to creative scholarship (1, p. 84). It aspires to offer all that can be institutionally offered, to the utmost reaches of late adolescent and early adult development; and whatever its limitations in other ways, a university college is in the best position to do this. The judgment will be hazarded, that when the intellect is that "objectively" represented by a Scholastic Aptitude rating of 650 or more, and the secondary school record is in proportion, the dice are loaded in favor of the good university college, and loaded against any but the most exacting of the autonomous colleges. For reasons later cited, there is no ground for thinking that "immaturity," or other out-of-line personality features, is any more of a liability in the university college than in the autonomous. If secondary school record is well below the above test-denoted expectation the university college is contraindicated, on the score of deficient motivation. There is another means of assessing this intellectual self-starting quality, as yet undeveloped, though the local Office of Tests has in progress some systematic research. This is essentially a refined intellectual evaluation of projective techniques. High-grade performance in this area largely offsets moderate "objective" scores, and to a lesser degree, mediocre secondary school record. In these circumstances such projective evidence is the best there is of potential intellect, which previous environments have simply not called out.

The other offerings of the university college are instrumental to making its intellectual ones effective. There is some tendency to look on them as less than those of the autonomous college (cf. 9, pp. 145 ff.). It is reasonable that this should be so, and where creative intellectual aspirations are not in the foreground, the case for the autonomous college is strong and will continue so. What, on the other hand, of the man who should be in a university college, such as Harvard, and is not? Only in exceptional circumstances can the autonomous college expect to maintain its previous relative status, especially in scientific areas (cf. 9, p. 144). Wastage of educational potentials at somewhat lower levels (e.g. higher education or not) has been comparatively easy to demonstrate, and this writer has commented on it elsewhere (5). Finer discriminations within higher education are possible, as between creative and absorptive intellects in various areas. Study of these differences, while critical for the individual case, remains at a "clinical" level; a simultaneous

Grant Study at a comparable autonomous college would by now have given it a more objective base. However, social implementations (should, therefore must, this man be at Harvard, Antioch, or Williams?) are not yet the official concern of a "free" society.

A question like the present cannot be dealt with apart from comparisons, such as just above. None of those here involved are to be taken as value-judgments beyond the sphere of expediency for the individual student. The "personalities" of colleges lend themselves to classification somewhat as do those of human individuals. Given suitable understanding in these terms of both student and college, and a healthy minded student, it is natural to think first of some college with which the student can readily "identify"; which is fairly close to the student's own temperamental setup. Explicitly or not, this seems to be a normal intention, and most mistakes that are made result from overestimating the like-mindedness of the two. The principle of *agere contra* is not excluded, but it must be an intelligently calculated risk.

Although they vary in similar dimensions, colleges are less subject to variation among each other than are individual students. No college could afford to have its stereotype as cyclothymic or as schizoid as it tolerates in its students, or in its faculty for that matter. Yet there are important differences in these limits of individual tolerance. A student personality may be so atypical as to bring about social rejection in a close-knit, autonomous college. In a large university college this rejection is unlikely to be so apparent or so real. Demands on conformity are less exigent; there is more time to assimilate corrective influences, as well as opportunity for better perspective upon them.

The most serious attempt so far at typing specific colleges—one that would bear considerable extension—was made over a decade ago by Fink and Cantril (2). Such features change with the years, and validity of the stereotype concept itself is limited, but the data are fully adequate to the present illustrative purposes. Comparisons were between Dartmouth, Harvard, Princeton, and Yale. Summating in the later Sheldonian (3) tripartite conceptions of temperament[1] the stereotype for Dartmouth was heavily (S), with comparatively slight (V) representation, and minimum of (C). For Harvard the stereotype was similarly dominated by (C) features, with slight development of the other two. For Princeton the main component was correspondingly (V), while for Yale it was again dominantly (S) but with considerable (V) admixture. It is doubtful if similar inquiry today would result differently in these main features. (A generation or more ago there was current a condensed typing for Bryn Mawr, Mt. Holyoke, Smith, Vassar, based on the questions (a) "Where does he go to church?" (b) "Who are his family?" (c) "What research is he doing?" (d) "Where is he?" Younger readers may do their own matching.)

From the standpoint of an individual selecting a college, the Fink-Cantril stereotypes and the above principle of temperamental identification, would from a Sheldonian standpoint be implemented as follows:

An institution of the Harvard stereotype is preferable in proportion to (a) the ascendance of (C), and (b) high entrance criteria, cf. the local Predicted Rank List. Perhaps the least indicative is a heavy (V) with moderate entrance criteria (though this combination has scarcely come to the writer's notice; corresponding (S) seems, by cases, to be not especially unfavorable).

An institution of the Yale or Princeton stereotype is preferable as (C) is lower than one or both of the other components. The Fink-Cantril data themselves point to the Yale stereotype where (S) is

---

[1] Viscerotonic-somatotonic-cerebrotonic. Cumbrousness in the terminology is unfortunate, but appears to be compensated by merits of content. Subsequent allusion to these trait-complexes is by initial letters (V), (S), (C). Grossly oversimplified, but as far as the three concepts can be represented in single words of ordinary usage, (V) = social, (S) = athletic, (C) = intellectual. Presumably every large college contains distinct student nuclei dominated by each of these patterns, whichever happens to dominate the general stereotype.

ascendant, to the Princeton stereotype where (V) is so. But to this writer, the two actual institutions have seemed closer together in these respects than the Fink-Cantril data place them.[2] At least among autonomous colleges, these (V) and (S) stereotypes may show more tolerance with respect to academic criteria. For high academic potentialities as such, the two type institutions would be in as good a position as any.

An institution of the Dartmouth stereotype is indicated where (S) is ascendant, and (C) traits are little developed. It is contraindicated for ascendant (C). The autonomous college relatively distant from larger population centers normally offers a somewhat different set of values from those presented in university colleges with close metropolitan contacts. In such autonomous institutions one may well expect less tolerance of deviations from a temperamental norm, besides more liberal policies with respect to academic entrance criteria.

Certain cases are now reviewed which have been presented in other settings, but where the present question was at least in the periphery. They point up divisions of the title question as follows:

1. Is (Harvard) the "one best bet" for this man, and why?
2. Is it a reasonably good bet, but should there be other places as good, perhaps better?
3. Should he probably not (have) come to (Harvard) and what other sort of place might be suggested?

Two previous presentations are considered: (4) dealing with Hygiene Department referral cases having adjustment problems in the presence of superior intellectual equipments; (5) concerning such referrals with indications of marginal intellectual equipment (plus two Grant Study cases of like psychometric status).

Without attempting individual mention of each case, it may be

---

[2] Thus from an old paraphrase of Kipling: ". . . There's times when you know they are lying—There's times when you think they are true—But there's things you will learn from the Orange and Black—That will help you a lot with the Blue."

said that among the superior intellects ($N = 28$) there were eight where the "one best bet" classification seems appropriate. An important basis for this seems to be a relative local tolerance for atypical trait-complexes provided they are associated with genuinely first-rate intellectual attainments. Thus, without skilled and sympathetic contacts seldom available in formal educational settings, Case XXXIII could well have become disorganized or antisocial, instead of as now, insightfully facing professional advancement limited only by the extent of conspicuous abilities in the given field. Case XXXV was having trouble; but it is ventured that in any other place he would have had more and earlier.

In eighteen cases no unsuitability of Harvard is suggested, but neither is any distinctive suitability. In one of these there was a specific suggestion of Yale, perhaps for a limited development of (C) traits.[3] In only two cases was there feeling that some other type of institution would have been clearly better. Both are in the "Lack of Purpose and Values" division of the cases. In Case L this is attested by severance for unsatisfactory work; an environment of more concrete demands, of which Antioch has become a higher-educational stereotype, suggested itself as more suitable. In Case LV the difficulty appears to have been of cyclothymic origin. In this case there was a technological orientation to which the liberal arts environment is less suited and which could (the therapeutic situation being equal) have given him a better balance than available in the local academic setting.

Of the twenty-eight cases in (5) half turned out by definition to be not good Harvard risks, as they did not academically survive there. From a constructive standpoint these fall into two groups. For eight cases an autonomous college is preferred, naturally one with less exacting academic requirements, though for three cases

---

[3] Cf. an anti-cerebrotonic monologue entitled "Why I sent my son to Yale"; now possibly forgotten, but current in the Harvard milieu about the beginning of the century, identifiable by the refrain, "Because I wanted him to be as popular as Tom Shevlin was."

there are specific suggestions respectively for an institution comparatively (S), (V), or (C). The last suggestion is more difficult to meet than the other two, but it could probably be done. For the remaining six cases it was felt that the junior college could meet any legitimate demands of "liberal" education. In four of the above fourteen, a technological trend could well have entered into plans.

Among the fourteen "survivors" were five of whom it was nevertheless thought that they would on temperamental grounds have got more from a well-chosen autonomous college. In five other cases it was felt that despite the marginal intellectual indications, Harvard could do as well by the student as the "next" college. The governing factors in this opinion appear to be strong intellectual motivation, relatively (C) temperament, and very well integrated personality, in various combinations. For the four remaining cases it actually seemed that no place quite as suitable as Harvard could be suggested. Here, in addition to the above factors, appears need for a particular type of emotional support locally well available, and distinctive response to the academic stimulations, such responsiveness as not commonly observed in students of the psychometric levels involved.

Certain cases appearing in a study of Harvard National Scholars (7) are of further relevance. This group is by definition selected for prospects of specially good adjustment to the local situation, naturally without prejudice to similar prospects elsewhere. Difficulties of present concern were encountered in seven of these cases and are in principle similar to those mentioned above. In three, possibly four of them, one would still say that Harvard was the most suitable place among the Fink-Cantril stereotypes. The difficulties represent unbalanced (C), with which the local institution is relatively well equipped to deal. If this trait complex fails here, the chances are that it would fail sooner and further elsewhere (cf. XXXV, above). When, however, it is associated with locally inadequate academic capacity, one may still think of an autonomous college carefully selected for (C) orientation.

In the remaining three cases the difficulty is rather of (S) origin, and this complex, in students of the present intellectual grade, would point in the direction of the Fink-Cantril stereotype for Yale. But in one case this component appeared so overweighted as to call into question the expediency of any liberal arts education.

A small number of cases are now reviewed in more detail, further to illustrate types of problems that arise in college selection and considerations that can be brought to bear on meeting them. The case numberings follow upon those in other papers based on similar material, in course of publication elsewhere (cf. 6, 7). There is relative emphasis on tests, since these were the main function of the writer's office. In descriptions of test data, the following verbal expressions denote scores *at least as good as* the following sigma distances from local means: Outstanding, $+ 1.25$; very superior, $+ 1.00$; superior, $+ .75$; well above average, $+ .50$; rather above average, $+ .25$; average, $- .25$; rather below average, $- .50$; well below average, $-.75$; inferior, -1.00; marginal, -1.25; submarginal, $- 1.50$.

Case CXXVII. This man was referred with respect to the presence of a "schizoid factor"; academic work undirected, much time spent in fantasy.

At entrance, SAT/MAT were both of outstanding grade, the latter somewhat higher. Secondary school work seems to have been of similar order. Predicted Rank, however, rated only well above average, and subject matter examinations as a whole only average; a marked disjunction but, in view of the general level, hardly enough to raise admission questions. At no time was class-room work much above average, or anywhere near what was implied in the Aptitude scores.

When first seen as above, formal test scores averaged at about the academic record reported, though the time for assimilating their instructions was at times submarginally long. Projective response was generally well developed with atypical content making a schizoid impression, "but not pathologically so." Rorschach responses tended to abstractions, with high level originals and organization. General demeanor was the least normal feature, with marked reduction of energy output, and mannerisms. This picture would fit the conception of schizoid, and in its setting could raise the question of a process.

Academic work continued at about average level, with referral for reexamination about a year afterwards. Then and later, formal intellectual scores remained about local average, coinciding with previous academic status. Projective work, if less rich, was on the whole more healthy than previously; general social impression was cited as distinctly better. Satisfactory academic status was not maintained; there was a brief period in the armed forces and of civilian employment of less exacting grade than initial endowment would denote. The history and test situation did not appear to justify his subsequent return here.

By the event, it may have been unwise for this man to have come to Harvard; but there was no basis in the available data for making such a judgment at the time of entrance. The most doubtful sign was the inconsistently low subject matter examination performance, which could not be governing. It is on the other hand probable that certain projective devices elsewhere mentioned would have given greater pause, perhaps sufficiently to turn the scale. This particular device has been aimed at intellectual functions not reached by "objective" tests. Here there had been no reason to suppose intellectual inadequacy and the procedure would have served its traditional function of indicating precautions on temperamental grounds. Still, any decision as close as this would also call for personal interview of fairly skilled level.

Prima facie, Harvard was as good a place as any for such a man; and if such a one does not make a go of it here, one can think of little else educationally than some simpler academic environment preferably not much loaded with (S). It is fairly certain that he met the first of these conditions, and possibly the second, at any rate there is later record of normal academic progress under the given circumstances. It looks now as if the schizoid features initially observed had largely subsided ("adolescent instability?") though the academic career is so far developing at a level rather below that of the original expectation. As above implied, there is no evidence that the earlier difficulties would have been avoided by having then gone to the place where he later adjusted normally.

Case CXXVIII. This man was referred with a history of erratic though on the whole above average college performance and a rather inadequate adaptation to armed service. On separation, the question of readmission is raised.

Pre-entrance tests had been erratic, like the subsequent academic performance. Globally, he had been accepted as a well below average risk. Submarginal SAT is associated with rather above average grade in a verbal entrance subject and with several honor grades in verbal college courses. Quantitative functions test consistently higher, but this is not reflected in college science grades.

When first seen, academic performance had averaged better than promise, as noted; but there remained the question as to the complete restoration of personality balance. General impression was "depressed, even exhausted." Test results uniformly favored technological rather than verbal work, but motivations are towards the verbal. The observations led to the opinion that (a) there were probably better places for him than Harvard, (b) it would be unwise to attempt its program at this time.

He had analytic therapy by a nonmedical practitioner with a first-rate background in psychology. Referral several months later notes marked improvement, recommendation for admission unless psychometric contraindications. No such were found, though there were further evidences of inadequate preparation, as a submarginal vocabulary score. The level of previous academic grades more than balances this. Readmission followed, with graduation in due course. Pretty much throughout there had been the advantage of a well-defined career plan. At last accounts, graduate work was progressing satisfactorily elsewhere.

The opinion set forth under (a) just above might be sustained from the standpoint of the local admitting authorities; from the standpoint of the student it was an error in principle, such as the viewpoint of this presentation may help to guard against (cf. Cases XXXIII, XXXV. It was apparently well advised that he continued applying to, and was later accepted by, this institution. Aside from his generally satisfactory work, the seemingly very effective therapy that he received would have been practicable in few if any other college surroundings. His career plan was one better suited to develop in the setting of a large university college, and though in this respect several other places would have been as well equipped, the temperamental milieu might well have been less suitable.

Case CXXIX. Referral cites own doubt about being in Harvard; marked cyclothymic episodes, temper outbursts; unstable family background. SAT-MAT both outstanding, but predicted rank scarcely average. Referral problem concerns personality type and degree of integration, also adaptability to literary career.

So far as tests are concerned such question would, in the light of previous information, be approached essentially from a projective angle. Available are such responses to pictures, to the Rorschach cards, the geometrical figures of previous allusion (4, p. 9 *et seq.;* also 8) and "what-would-happen-if" questions. In none of these was the productivity more than mediocre. Positive evidence for intellectual productivity thus fails to turn up, and the fact that this is the case over a range of differentially affect-laden techniques argues rather against repressive dynamics.

Quoting from remarks at the time, "Sheldon would probably put somatotonia first, and cerebrotonia fairly well up. . . . Kempf would put him among his hyperkinetics, indeed . . . a type specimen for this group . . . sophisticated aggressiveness makes one think of Wilson Mizner as a prototype, though one does not find here evidence of Mizner's intellectual talent . . . possibly a more somatotonic college like ——— would be in a better position. . . ."

From a further projective standpoint, note was also made of a script singularly disordered for one of this educational status. As above, there is nothing to presage intellectual productivity of a high level, but a popular level might well be attained and sustained through the unusual energic capacity. There would be no doubt of his intellectual powers to master the Harvard undergraduate program. From an organismic standpoint there are probably several institutions that would have been wiser selections for him. There is no special object in a university college for such a man. There would be a risk that in a heavily (S) environment this component would get away from him. "One would wish for at least as much (V) in his surroundings, such as this writer somehow fancies might be provided by ———, for example."

Case CXXX. This man was first referred as a studied nonconformist, living much in the past, reacting poorly to competitive situations, for whatever light a general psychometric scrutiny might throw on the situation. It may be observed that prima facie this picture is one that should find fewer adjustment difficulties locally than in most colleges.

SAT outstanding, MAT marginal. Despite a one-sidedness of intellectual development, as above, and atypical behavior observed, a favorable impression was made on both social and intellectual grounds, the latter mainly on a projective basis, reinforcing the previous (verbal) multiple choice findings. Adjustment difficulties were predicted, but enough "basic personality strength" was estimated for managing them without breakdown.

He was psychiatrically judged at this time to be "pretty upset" over anxiety-producing situations such as approaching examinations. Actually he did not meet these challenges but remained out of college for several months, being then referred a second time as to readmission. The impression was then somewhat less favorable; a comparatively rich Rorschach response of previous record is now on the constricted side. A verbal alpha series was only rather above local average, with number functions submarginal. Certain spatial and reasoning tests, based on Kuhlmann-Binet, were erratic, but globally within reasonable limits. Word-association was fairly rapid as might be expected, but in content neutral.

He did not return at this time but the question was again raised some three years later, the interval having been spent in relevant pursuits. The impression is rather that of the interview just previous. Rorschach and Circle (8) responses are still constricted for one of his intellectual history, particularly where artistic interests are much in the foreground (present Rorschach W:D, however, is 1:1.7 against previous 1:5). It is problematical if the type of motivation now evident is sufficient to sustain the intellectual powers at the level demanded by local standards. He was thought to be within an "acceptable range," though scarcely an average risk, contrary to the initial impression. At that time potentialities were there, and if this situation can be restored, this is an environment favorable enough for him. As things look now, a better bet for him would probably be an autonomous college oriented in the direction of his well-defined interests; but the odds are within reason, on both sides. The event will prove.

Case CXXXI. When first seen, this man was referred on the question of readmission. There was a history of rather more than satisfactory academic performance for two years; then a major psychosis of a few months' duration, with the immediate question of whether he was sufficiently stabilized for readmission.

Entrance tests were adequate but erratic; later course grades better than they would have predicted. A similar erratic tendency appeared in the narrower context of the immediate test observations; some verbal speed tests ranging from more than 1.25 sigma above to more than 1.00 sigma below the local mean. The verbal subtests of the Wechsler-Bellevue were used for their qualitative features, though they are not particularly discriminating as high as this. Global score was actually about ninety-eighth percentile, with the best work in the critical Similarities subtest. Owing to Rorschach sophistication, another series of the type was used. Response was regarded as "a little constricted and unusual, but need not have been at all disturbed."

Social impression was of relative affectation, but discounted for different background. It was felt that no proper obstacle to readmission existed in the observations. Referring authorities apparently decided on postponement, and he was seen again several months later. The psychometric work was if anything more erratic than previously, though from a global standpoint there could be little question of intellectual adequacy. Behaviorally the impression was less good than previously but he was given benefit of the doubt and readmitted. Stability was not preserved and a brief period of hospitalization was again necessary, raising the question of the wisdom of his continuing. He appeared symptom-free when seen psychometrically for the third time. The general intellectual level was as previously, locally adequate, but not especially superior. Behaviorally the impression was considerably better, with expressions of good insight and plans for reorganization of life.

In the absence of the history, status at this time could hardly have been a bar to readmission; but with it, one has to weigh this man's potentialities against other users of the educational facilities. If the potentialities had been those of Case CXVII (7) for example, the risk might have been acceptable, though the psychiatric outlook seems not quite so good for this case. Under the conditions, readmission did not seem justified from the institution's standpoint, and it is similarly questionable if the risk was a wise one for the man himself. Not enough is known about the genesis of conditions like his for more than an educated guess at the role of the academic surroundings in precipitating the upsets. For whatever role they may have, the local situation is probably not the best for such a person. There should be a better chance of his keeping balance in the simpler environment of a nonmetropolitan, autonomous college, with (S) subordinated to the other two components. Work of a graduate level is hardly in the psychometric picture, though previous academic grades are not inconsistent with it.

Case CXXXII. The specific problem of referral concerned aptitude for engineering training; evidence for such aptitude already existed and from this standpoint the function was essentially one of checking.

The principal areas of such an inquiry are the mathematical, mechanical, and spatial. There was previous indication of a strong mathematical bias, SAT score being marginal and MAT outstanding. Tests given at secondary school had testified specially for engineering training. Entrance examinations in verbal areas had been not far from local average, but secondary school work in general had been less than mediocre, contributing to a Predicted Rank of not even "submarginal" level.

Verbal tests undertaken here had generally marginal scores. For the mathematical-mechanical-spatial complex, scores were spotty, ranging from submarginal (DAT Abstract Reasoning) to outstanding (Thurstone PMA Number Series Completion), with the weight heavily in this latter direction. The profile of the scores presents from the standpoint of scatter-analysis a puzzle whose discussion is outside the present scope. The general situation was one in which projective responses might be expected to show disturbance. In a condensed Rorschach procedure there was some development of white-space and marked development of Vista; a good deal of CF, with various disorganization on the color cards.

The Vistas however were of good level and the pattern cannot be termed at all "constricted."

Aside from test data, conscious motivations are strongly towards engineering. The student's presence at this institution is not his own choice. A frequent case can be made out for basing the training of the professional engineer upon a liberal arts foundation, and institutions have adapted their curricula to this fact. It is not, however, one to be made the basis of a general policy. To be applicable in this case, one would have wanted qualities implicit in, for instance, an SAT of at least superior level instead of marginal, a vocabulary rating of at least superior instead of well below average, as well as better organized projective response than was shown. According to both test indications and accessible dynamic factors, this student should not be at Harvard or any like institution, but at a high-level, while strictly oriented, technological school.

Given the situation above, it is a legitimate question if an institution like Harvard is not justified in declining to admit on the specific ground of far better adaptability to a different type of education.

Case CXXXIII. The referral problem here is simply that of whether the young man, now well along in a reputable secondary school, should plan coming to Harvard. The case itself is a relatively clear-cut one. The young fellow is a pattern of benign (S), minimally ectomorphic, for whom, according to various other intrinsic factors, one might think first of Yale, Dartmouth, or Notre Dame. Only factors extrinsic to his personality would be likely to put Harvard in first place. Psychometrically, the Bellevue verbal subtests summated to about a ninetieth percentile and would vote against the more exacting liberal arts colleges, the more so as the lowest subtest standard score is for Similarities, 10. Submarginal scores appear in other abstracting functions, verbal and spatial. Rorschach response is of interest from a "striving" standpoint; their number is nearly 2 sigma high, and there are over twelve times as many D's as W's, practically all F's.

Upon such evidence, this student should find various more suitable channels for intellectual development and Harvard better educational risks. The average autonomous college would offer a fair chance of graduating, and there are probably several that would be glad to get someone of his physique and temperament. Conceding the desirability of further liberal arts education, the junior college should be capable of meeting needs such as these. In view of the strongly marked temperament, however, it may be questioned whether even so much concession is wise. The benign somatotonic is almost by definition motivated towards the maintenance and advancement of people's physical well-being. This is stuff of which good athletic directors are often made. There should be no difficulty in meeting the formal requirements of this type of training, whereas there would probably be a good deal if one carried this interest to the level of medical education. There is, incidentally, evidence of fairly active ideational life when hooked up with (S) themes.

Recurring now to the previous three-fold division of the selection problem ("one best bet," etc.), in terms of highly suitable, suitable, comparatively unsuitable: in the light of present information, for none of these seven cases can Harvard be cited as highly suitable. For the first three, Harvard can be rated as suitable, though not necessarily the most so. For the remaining four, it appears comparatively unsuitable. Reasons for these estimates are, however, essentially dissimilar, varying with the intellectual and temperamental situation; and a present estimate needs to be qualified in terms of what information was, or could have been, available at the time of college selection. Thus, in the case of CXXVII, rather careful scrutiny at the time of entrance put him well within the highly suitable category from the standpoint of the institution, and even more clearly so from his own standpoint. Closer observation might have modified the case for him with the institution, but hardly for the institution with him.

In CXXVII above, intellectual equipment was ample, but modified by marked, if passing, temperamental difficulties. In CXXVIII intellectual equipment is less, but the temperamental difficulties came under relatively successful management. Harvard could hardly have regarded itself as a more than "suitable" risk for this man, though from his standpoint it seems fortunate that he came. Motivation was prima facie superior, in view of the formulated career plan.

CXXIX contrasts heavily with these two: higher intellectual capacity than either, and rather less motivation in this respect. Plus the predominance of (S) one can say that he is "suitable" for the local institution, but scarcely that he has been best advised to choose it. That is, for CXXVII there would have been no place so suitable; for CXXVIII there were probably places at least as suitable, for CXXIX there were probably places more suitable though not critically so. Temperament well outweighs intellectual factors in these estimates.

In CXXX there is career interest as definite as CXXVIII's, but it is less easy to integrate with the local academic discipline and seems to be on a level of emotion rather than "conation." There is not the energy output of CXXIX or the intellectual sensibility of CXXVII. There is more (V) component than in any case here mentioned, and the type of intellect is suitable only under better general integrations than appear. Better solutions for such a type of man are to be found among the autonomous colleges, and it seems that this estimate could have been made earlier, with closer scrutiny.

For CXXXI there was the immediate question of whether the existing stability warranted the local program, which as noted was decided negatively. But as with CXXVII there is the broader question whether closer scrutiny would have anticipated this decision at entrance. With CXXVII it is likely that projective techniques would have paid off; with CXXXI this is less likely. A good psychiatric history might have set up warning signals. In none of the other cases has there been the intercurrent change of college suitability that appears here, and it seems, for practical purposes, of an unpredictable character.

CXXXII presents an overtly clear-cut situation of extrinsic pressures operating against well-defined and consistent aptitudes and career motivations. The case exhibited less psychiatric background than any of the series except CXXXIII, and suggested that the institution might reasonably safeguard both itself and applicants against complications of this nature.

Of these latter four cases, for which Harvard is estimated as "comparatively unsuitable," CXXXIII is perhaps the best defined. As such, a heavy (S) component, no matter how healthy, rather contraindicates the liberal arts, though it is compatible enough with them when associated with outstanding intellect (CXXIX) and/or with well-developed (C) as in various Grant Study cases. Here, neither of these conditions was observed and the suggested program is based on the benign (S) which is so distinctive a feature of this personality.

Six basic types of college choice present themselves: (a) the university or autonomous college, (b) as the institution's temperamental pattern is dominated by (V), (S), or (C) features. There is the additional factor of "scholastic aptitude"; as noted, the offerings of the university college are believed relatively to increase as this aptitude moves into the upper reaches. In this respect, the common estimate of the better-known institutions appears valid enough for any normal situation. The principal chances for "idiographic" error appear to be (a) misestimating the value of liberal arts education (as against, e.g., technological) for a particular case, (b) mistaken choice by or for the student of a milieu with an incompatible temperamental pattern.[4] There appears to be a recent instance in which this latter cost the student his life.

The above case-accounts have, by definition, dealt with situations where the suitability of the student for the local environment was in doubt. There have been many statements of the objectives of higher education, of the qualities one would like to see emerge from the experience of this environment. A group selected in the manner of the Grant Study participants should have a good representation of personalities embodying them. Someone may later give case-accounts to illustrate these men, such as those exemplified in the Study's serial designations of 24, 54, 137, 185, 238, 254. A university college need have no higher aspiration level than to make and keep itself a place where such men should have been.

REFERENCES

1. *Report on Some Problems of Personnel in the Faculty of Arts and Sciences.* (Prepared by a special committee appointed by the President of Harvard University). Cambridge: Harvard University Press, 1939.
2. FINK, K., and CANTRIL, H.: "The collegiate stereotype as frame of reference." *J. Abnorm. Soc. Psychol.,* 1937, *32:* 352–356.
3. SHELDON, W. H., and STEVENS, S. S.: *The Varieties of Temperament: A Psychology of Constitutional Differences.* New York: Harper & Brothers, 1942.
4. WELLS, F. L.: "Psychometric patterns in adjustment problems at upper extremes of test 'intelligence': Cases XXIX–LVI." *J. Genetic Psychol.,* 1950, *76:* 3–37.
5. WELLS, F. L.: "College survivals and non-survivals at marginal test levels: Cases LVII–LXXXIV." *J. Genetic Psychol.,* 1950, *77:* 153–185.

---

[4] A suggestion of immediate pertinence for the student is to interview from this standpoint those personnel officers of large organizations "who devote all their time or a large fraction of it to the hiring of college graduates. Here he can get a broad view of a large number of institutions, since these men visit the institutions year after year . . ." (Francis J. Curtis in *Chemical Engineering News,* 1950, *28:* 2422.)

6. WELLS, F. L.: "Rorschach and Bernreuter procedures with Harvard National Scholars in the Grant Study: Cases III, IX, X, XXVII, XXVIII, CIII–CXII." *J. Genetic Psychol.,* in press.

7. WELLS, F. L.: "Further notes on Rorschach and Case History in Harvard National Scholars: Cases CXIII–CXXVI." *J. Genetic Psychol.,* in press.

8. WELLS, F. L.: "Some projective functions of simple geometrical figures: Cases LXXXV–XCV." *J. Genetic Psychol.,* 1950, *77:* 187–210.

9. WHITE, LYNN, JR.: *Educating Our Daughters.* New York: Harper & Brothers, 1950.

7

Twenty Year Follow-up of
Medical Interests

Edward K. Strong, Jr.

Stanford University

At the final dinner of the disbanded Division of Psychology at Carnegie Institute of Technology, in the spring of 1923, Walter V. Bingham, head of the Division, reviewed the many achievements of the Division. In response to a question as to what had probably been the outstanding achievement of the Division, he stated that in his opinion the measurement of interests by Yoakum, Moore, Ream, and Freyd would prove to be more significant in the future than any other phase of the Division's contributions to applied psychology.

The writer does not pretend that he has given exactly the right wording or coloring to Bingham's statement, but does remember that he was surprised to hear Bingham so speak. At that time too little had been accomplished to make certain that interests were significant in human behavior or that they could be measured satisfactorily. In contrast, outstanding achievements had been made in intelligence testing, job analysis, rating scales, and the selection and training of salesmen and department store personnel. The Retail Institute, transferred to the University of Pittsburgh that year, and the Life Insurance Sales Research Bureau, already organized in 1922, resulted from part of the early work of the Division and have continued to function to the present time. Many, many other developments would need to be listed in order to give a proper idea of what had been done, and what was to be achieved, as a result of the Division's activities. To say then that the origination of interest measurement was the most significant accomplishment was surprising to say the least.

The writer is sure that Bingham's remarks influenced his thinking. He is also certain that many arguments on the subject between Freyd and himself helped fixate the matter in his mind. Anyway, the first assignment made to a graduate student upon arrival at Stanford University in the fall of 1923 was to Karl M. Cowdery to see how well he could differentiate engineers, lawyers, and physicians from one another, using Freyd's interest blank.

Cowdery's success, coupled with his evident intention not to follow up the research, left the writer with insatiable curiosity as to how far it was possible to differentiate occupational groups from one another on the basis of interests and what such differentiation could contribute to vocational guidance. After twenty-seven years of working on one idea after another, the writer is still interested in many new phases of the subject undreamed of in early days.

The report that follows gives additional proof that occupational groups can be differentiated in terms of interests, that the interests of men while in college are closely associated with the occupations actually engaged in twenty years later, and that interests disclose a much larger sector of the total personality than has hitherto been appreciated.

The predictability of interest scores is considered in terms of students who became physicians. Comparisons are made between such students and those who entered other occupations. The results show that the two groups are well differentiated and that the future physicians scored, on the average, 96 per cent as high as could be expected.

TWENTY-YEAR FOLLOW-UP

Data on three groups of Stanford University students are considered here. First, 306 college freshmen tested on the Vocational Interest Test in 1927 and 202 of them retested in 1949. Second, 285 seniors tested in 1927 and 218 retested in 1949. Third, 304 graduate students tested in 1927 and 199 retested in 1949. Almost exactly 80 per cent of each group replied in 1949 of those still alive and whose addresses were known. Many of these students were also tested once or twice at intervals between 1927 or 1930 and 1949. Extensive information has also been obtained as to each man's occupational career and his reactions to the occupations in which he has been engaged.

Two sets of occupational interest scores are considered—the test scores while in college and the retest scores in 1949.

Two occupations for each man are also considered—his occupational choice when first tested and the occupation in which he was engaged in 1949.

The students' records have been contrasted in three different ways. First, whether they had high or low scores on the physician interest scale while students. Second, whether they were practicing medicine in 1949 or engaged in some other occupation. Third, whether they continued in the occupation of their choice while in college or shifted subsequently to some other occupation.

The objective of these three comparisons is to obtain measures of how far occupational interest scores while in college predict the occupation engaged in twenty years later.

It should be noted that the records pertain to Stanford University students who must have a high scholastic record in order to be admitted and for the most part possess sufficient intelligence to enter almost any occupation. We would not expect as good a prediction for all men as reported here since general abilities would play relatively a more important role among all men than among these college men.

"The criterion of a vocational interest test should be whether or not the person will be satisfied in the career to which it directs him, other factors than interest being disregarded." Since the scoring procedure indicates whether or not one has the interests of men who are engaged in the occupation, it follows that the validity of such a test "should be measured in terms of satisfaction, not while the person is preparing for the work but later on while he is actually engaged therein" (1, p. 384).

Although the writer still believes that the validity of an interest test should be measured in terms of satisfaction on the job, he feels that there is no satisfactory measure of satisfaction at the present time and because of this condition it is preferable to substitute for satisfaction the criterion of being engaged in the occupation.

A man's occupational career is the resultant of many factors besides interest. Consequently we cannot expect perfect agreement between interest scores and occupations engaged in. As there is no way of estimating the effect of the many factors upon selection of a career there is no way of knowing whether interests can contribute 20, 40, 60, or 80 per cent of the total. Since we do not know how much interests should contribute to the total we cannot estimate how effective the Vocational Interest Test is as a device for measuring interests. The information given below as to the relationship which exists between interest scores while in college and occupation engaged in twenty years later is useful as it indicates what degree of prediction can be expected from interest scores and furthermore it is an aid in future calculations as to how much other factors, such as economic conditions, family pressures, available finances, etc., affect a man's occupational career.

If interests completely determined a man's occupational career and if the Vocational Interest Test completely measured occupational interests, then the following propositions should be true.

1. Students who have a high physician interest score become physicians and those with low scores do not become physicians.

2. Students who become physicians score while in college like physicians and those who do not become physicians do not score like physicians.

3. Students who choose a medical career and subsequently change to some other occupation (a) do not score as high in physician interest as students who do not change and (b) score higher in their second occupation than in medicine.

4. Students who choose a nonmedical career and subsequently change to medicine (a) do not score as high in the nonmedical interest as students who continue therein and (b) score higher in medicine than in the occupation of their first choice.

Consider now how far the above propositions are true.

PROPOSITION I: STUDENTS WITH HIGH PHYSICIAN INTEREST SCORES BECOME PHYSICIANS AND THOSE WITH LOW SCORES DO NOT BECOME PHYSICIANS

The distribution of physician interest scores for 670 freshmen, seniors, and graduate students is given in Table I. The distribution of such scores for the 108 students who became physicians and the distribution for the remaining 562 students who did not become physicians are given in the second and third columns of the table. The former average 47.3 and the latter 29.7, a very large difference.

The mean score of nonphysicians closely approximates the mean chance score of 29.2 on this scale.

Among these 670 students there is 100 per cent chance of becoming a physician with a score of 70 on the physician scale, 67 per cent chance with a score of 60 to 69, 62 per cent chance with a score of 50 to 59, down to 4 per cent chance with a score of 25 to 29, and less than 0.5 per cent with scores below 25 (see the last column of Table

TABLE I. Distribution of Physician Interest Scores of College Students

(Classified according to occupation engaged in 20 years later)

Physician Rating	Scale Score	Total (670)	Physicians (108)	Non-physicians (562)	Dentists, Biologists (18)	Psychologists (9)	Chemists (12)	Engineers (65)	Lawyers (72)	Salesmen (22)	Chance of being a Physician
A	70	1	1	—	—	—	—	—	—	—	100
	65	3	2	1	1	—	—	—	—	—	67
	60	6	4	2	1	—	—	—	—	—	67
	55	19	15	4	2	1	—	—	—	—	79
	50	44	24	20	6	1	1	3	1	—	55
	45	60	24	36	5	2	5	5	3	2	40
B+	40	70	14	56	3	2	—	10	5	—	20
B	35	83	10	73	—	—	4	13	3	1	12
B−	30	82	9	73	—	—	—	11	12	1	11
C+	25	91	4	87	—	2	—	11	12	2	4
C	20	74	0	74	—	—	—	6	10	3	0
	15	82	1	81	—	—	1	6	18	6	0
	10	35	—	35	—	—	—	—	3	5	0
	5	13	—	13	—	—	—	—	4	2	0
	0	6	—	6	—	—	—	—	1	—	0
	−5	1	—	1	—	—	—	—	—	—	0
Mean		32.5	47.3	29.7	51.4	41.9	40.4	34.0	25.7	21.4	
Sigma		13.4	9.8	12.1	6.6	10.2	10.3	9.4	10.7	11.1	
% Overlapping		—	—	42	83	79	73	49	30	21	
Correlation		—	—	—	.80	.74	.73	.52	.16	.53	

I). In terms of ratings the chances are 53 per cent with an A rating, 20 per cent with a B+ rating, 12 per cent with a B rating, 11 per cent with a B— rating, and less than 2 per cent with a C rating.

The 670 students have entered many different occupations, let us say one hundred different occupations. On that basis the chance that any one would go into medicine is 1 per cent. If, however, they have an A rating on the physician scale there is a 53 per cent chance they will become a physician!

Low scores on most psychological tests are more predictive than high scores. There are few chances one will become a physician if he has a low score on that scale, but there is only about 1 chance in 2 that he will become a physician if he has a high score. Many who desire to become physicians are unable to do so for lack of ability or of finances. Some choose related activities, related in the sense that the interests of men in the related occupations correlate highly with the interests of physicians.

The interests of dentists correlate .87 with the interests of physicians and we should guess that the interests of biologists would correlate at least .80 with those of physicians. The physician interest scores of two students who became dentists and the sixteen students who became biologists are given in column four of the table. (This group actually averages higher than those who became physicians— 51.4 versus 47.3.) A high score on the physician scale did not result in these eighteen men becoming physicians but one cannot claim that their becoming dentists or biologists represents a serious disagreement between interest scores and occupation-engaged-in. Including these 18 biologists with the 108 physicians gives a 64 per cent chance that an A rating on the physician scale will lead to the man becoming a physician, dentist, or biologist. When all the factors involved in vocational selection are considered, a 64 per cent chance is extremely high.

The interests of architects, psychologists, and chemists correlate with the interests of physicians between .70 and .80. Eleven of the

TABLE II. DISTRIBUTION OF PHYSICIAN INTEREST SCORES RELATIVE TO OCCUPATION ENGAGED IN

Scale	r	Typical Occupations	Physician Interest Scores					
			60 to 70	55 to 59	50 to 54	45 to 49	40 to 44	10 to −5
15	.90	Physician	7	14	25	24	14	—
12	.83	Dentist, biologist	2	0	2	3	2	—
9	.72	Architect, psychologist, chemist	—	1	2	8	7	1
6	.54	Engineer, writer, geologist	—	1	8	9	19	2
3	.29	Economist, farmer, ind. engineer	1	2	1	2	7	3
0	0	Math-sci. teacher, advertiser, lawyer	—	—	2	6	10	11
−3	−.29	CPA, production mgr.	—	—	1	3	3	3
−6	−.54	Salesman, retail wholesale	—	—	1	4	4	17
−9	−.72	Accountant, banker, office man	—	—	2	1	1	12
N			10	18	44	60	67	49
Mean of scale scores			13.3	12.9	10.3	8.4	6.4	−3.1
Sigma			3.3	4.0	6.6	6.9	6.1	4.6
Percentage who become physicians			70	78	57	40	21	0
Percentage physicians or biologists			90	78	61	45	24	0
Percentage physicians or related occupations			90	89	84	73	63	6

remaining 40 A ratings on the physician scale are found among men who entered these three occupations. A few of the nonphysicians who rated A have entered an occupation which correlates about zero and even distinctly negative. This is illustrated from data of those who became lawyers (correlation of .16) and salesmen (correlation of —.53). Four lawyers and two salesmen among 94 have an A rating on the physician scale.

In order to show in a fairly simple manner that, as scores go down on the physician scale, there are fewer and fewer men found in medical and related occupations and more and more men found in nonrelated occupations, Table II is presented. A scale from 15 to —9 is used in terms of z scores to represent the correlations between interests of physicians and other occupations. The occupations of the students have been rated by the writer and two other psychologists from 15 for physicians to —9 for office workers and sales managers whose interests correlate about —.70 with the interests of physicians. The occupations of most students were assigned a rating with confidence; for a few cases the rating is a rough guess but probably not wrong by more than one step on the scale used in the table. If a man has a score of 60 to 70 on the physician scale he enters on the average an occupation with a scale rating of 13.3; if his score is 55 to 59, his occupation has a scale rating of 12.9; if his score is 50–54, his occupation has a rating of 10.3, etc. The trend is unmistakable that the higher he scores on the physician scale, the more the occupation he enters will be related to that of medicine. There are, however, a few physicians who had low scores while in college and a few more nonphysicians who had high scores at that time.

PROPOSITION 2: STUDENTS WHO BECOME PHYSICIANS SCORE WHILE IN COLLEGE LIKE PHYSICIANS AND THOSE WHO DO NOT BECOME PHYSICIANS DO NOT SCORE LIKE PHYSICIANS

Mean scores of all freshmen, seniors, and graduate students who planned to be physicians and became so are given in Table III.

TABLE III. MEAN PHYSICIAN INTEREST SCORES OF STUDENTS WHO PLANNED TO BE PHYSICIANS

	Freshmen						Seniors						Graduate Students					
	Complete Records			Complete & Incomplete			Complete Records			Complete & Incomplete			Complete Records			Complete & Incomplete		
Year	N	M	σ	N	M	σ	N	M	σ	N	M	σ	N	M	σ	N	M	σ
1927	13	43.6	9.4	29	43.7	10.7	11	48.8	5.7	20	48.5	6.4	44	47.1	9.2	78	48.9	10.3
1930	13	42.9	8.3	23	43.8	10.3												
1931																		
1932							11	54.3	9.2	16	52.5	9.2	44	48.9	9.7	58	52.4	9.3
1937							11	52.0	11.5	15	52.1	10.3						
1939	13	48.6	7.4	19	49.8	8.1												
1949	13	45.2	7.7	23	45.3	11.5	11	52.0	11.5	16	51.8	10.2	44	49.8	9.1	53	50.1	9.9

There are complete records from 68 of these men—complete in the sense that the freshmen and seniors filled out the Vocational Interest Test four times and reported each time their occupational career and the graduate students did so on three occasions. There are in addition a varying number of additional cases that failed to reply on one, two, or three occasions. These incomplete records are combined with the complete records and reported in the table. It is apparent that the incomplete records do not differ appreciably from the complete records. The combined data are therefore used as they represent larger samples and at the same time all of our cases.

The freshmen naturally were three years younger than the seniors and had not yet started premedical work. The seniors, on the other hand, for the most part were taking the premedical program when first tested, although a minority were engaged in a nonmedical program as undergraduates. The fact that the freshmen score lower than the seniors (43.2 versus 48.0, critical ratio of only 2.0) can be explained as due to less maturity—interests change somewhat from age 19 to 22—or to nonentrance into medical training. A third explanation is more plausible, namely, that the freshman group contains one or two more men with low physician interest than a normal sample. This explanation is supported by the fact that the freshmen also score lower than the seniors in 1949 (44.8 versus 51.5, critical ratio of 2.0).

All the students reported in Table III said they were planning to be physicians when first tested. There are in addition five cases that reported they did not know what they were going to do, and four cases that reported they were going to enter some occupation other than medicine, both subgroups eventually becoming physicians. These two small groups average, respectively, 49.8 and 38.0 on the physician scale. When these 9 cases are combined with the 127 cases of freshmen, seniors, and graduate students, we obtain the mean score of 47.6 for the first test and 49.1 for the 1949 retest.

How good are such results? How well do interest scores of

students foretell that they will become physicians? One way of answering such questions is to compare the students' scores with those of the criterion group. The distributions of such scores are given in Table IV. It is evident that the two distributions closely agree, supported by the chi square P of .30.

TABLE IV. DISTRIBUTION OF PHYSICIAN INTEREST SCORES IN PERCENTAGES

Physician Interest Score	Criterion Group (N=331)	Students (N=137)
70	0.3	0.8
65	3.6	2.9
60	10.6	5.1
55	20.5	15.3
50	21.5	20.4
45	13.6	19.7
40	12.1	12.4
35	8.4	10.2
30	4.8	8.0
25	3.9	4.4
20	0.3	0.0
15	0.3	0.8
Mean	50.0	47.6
σ	10.0	10.3

In counseling it is customary to recommend to students that they seriously consider all occupations on which they obtain an A rating and less seriously their B + ratings. Lower scores are usually ignored. On this basis 70 per cent of the criterion group and 64 per cent of the students would be urged to consider medicine and 12 per cent more of both groups to take the profession under consideration. On the other hand 17 per cent of the criterion group and 23 per cent of the students would not have had medicine recommended to them. Use of the interest test means that 17 per cent of men who practice medicine would not be doing so if they had relied on the test. We can not declare that the interest test is ineffective in 17 per cent of cases because there is no way of determining whether or not the 17 per cent would have been more successful and satisfied if they had entered some other occupation upon which they had scored higher than on medicine. It is of course probable that the interest test is not perfect in the sense that true physician interests are not perfectly measured on the present scale. And it is also probable that some men may be relatively more successful and satisfied in a profession which affords a good income and high social prestige in contrast to other occupations for which they have greater interest but which would relegate them to lower income and less prestige.

Taking the above into account and especially that one of every six men who are physicians score below B +, is there some way in which the scores of students may be compared with those of the criterion and the comparison be expressed not in two distributions, as in Table IV, but in one measure of efficiency?

The maximum mean score on any occupational scale is 50, the mean of a criterion group on its own scale. Considering the size of our physician criterion group we estimate that a second criterion group would average not 50 on our present scale but about 49.2 (1, p. 647). This latter figure is then the maximum mean score actually to be expected. The average of the scores lowest on each blank is 4.4 for 285 seniors in 1927. This score of 4.4 is the minimum mean score that any group could obtain. Actually to obtain a mean score of 4.4 on the chemist scale, for example, we would have to select men who had interests diametrically opposed to those of chemists. The interests of life insurance agents correlate — .84 with the interests of chemists. Actually life insurance agents average 9.9 on the chemist scale. If we had a group that correlated — 1.00, not — .84, with the interests of chemists we might obtain a mean score of 4.4. The mean chance score on the physician scale is 29.1, approximately half way between 49.2 and 4.4. To the extent that a chance score should occur midway between the two extremes it affords somewhat of an independent check on the two extreme landmarks.

Calling the score of 4.4 zero efficiency and 49.2 100 per cent efficiency, we have a scale on which can be expressed how well our students scored in terms of the occupation of medicine which they entered. When in college the freshmen scored 88 per cent of the maximum, the seniors 98 per cent, the graduate students 99 per cent, and all combined 96 per cent (see Table V). The percentages

TABLE V. EFFICIENCY PERCENTAGES OF MEAN PHYSICIAN INTEREST SCORES

		Test	Retest
29	Freshmen	88	91
20	Seniors	98	105
78	Graduate Students	99	102
136	Total *	96	99

* Total includes 9 additional cases (see text).

of efficiency are 3 to 7 per cent higher in 1949, about twenty years later.

In this article the data are restricted to the medical profession. In another article (2) the data include medicine and many other occupations in which the students are now engaged. In this latter article the percentage of efficiency averages 92 per cent in college and 95 per cent in 1949. No one can ask more than this for any test.

Mean scores represent the absolute size of interest scores. Their relative rank needs to be considered, since in counseling a man's highest scores are given preferment and this is true whether his three highest scores are all above 50 or are all between 40 and 44.

Some men have many high scores, some have no A ratings (scores of 45 and higher). The means given above are based on scores where in a minority of cases a score of 44, or 41, or even lower, is the man's highest score. A score of 41 is not high and lowers the mean of the group below 50 but if it is the man's highest score it is given preference on that account. Consider Freshman #110. His five highest scores are

1930		1931		1939		1949	
Realtor	41	Physician	52	Physician	56	Lawyer	48
Musician	40	Dentist	47	Lawyer	48	Physician	47
Office man	40	Lawyer	45	Mathematician	46	Mathematician	43
Physician	38	Author	42	Author	46	Author	43
Lawyer	38	Musician	41	Architect	43	Architect	42

Here the score of physician has varied from 38 to 52, 56, and 47. The rank has varied from 4.5 to 1, 1, and 2. The score in 1930 is low, only a B rating, in comparison with the A ratings in the three retests. Nevertheless because it was within three of the highest score it should be seriously considered as the occupation to enter.

TABLE VI. MEDIAN RANK OF PHYSICIAN INTEREST SCORES *

Year	Freshmen			Seniors			Graduate Students		
	N	Med.	Q	N	Med.	Q	N	Med.	Q
1927				20	2.1	1.6	44	2.2	2.2
1930	29	3.6	3.9						
1931	23	3.8	4.2						
1932				16	2.8	1.2	44	1.7	2.0
1937				15	1.8	2.1			
1939	19	1.7	2.0						
1949	23	2.8	4.1	16	1.5	1.6	44	2.2	1.7

* Data correspond to those in Table III for combined complete and incomplete records except for graduate students (where only complete records are considered here). Many of the blanks of the incomplete records have not yet been scored except on the physician scale.

The physician scores of freshmen ranked 3.6 highest in 1930 and rose to 2.8 in 1949 (see Table VI). The corresponding medians for seniors are 2.1 and 1.5 and for graduate students 2.2 and 2.2. When an occupational interest score is ranked among thirty-four, the chance median rank is seventeen. Median ranks of 3.6 to 1.5 are far removed from what chance would give.

Students who become physicians score like physicians on the first test while in college and score slightly higher on the retest about twenty years later. This does not mean that every individual has an A rating on both occasions. If they did they would average far higher than the criterion group, for 12 per cent of the latter rate B + and 17 per cent rate lower than B +. When we say that students who became physicians score like adult physicians we recognize that a small minority of both groups score low on the physician scale but on the average students score 96 per cent as high as adult physicians.

PROPOSITION 3: STUDENTS WHO CHOOSE A MEDICAL CAREER AND SUBSE-QUENTLY CHANGE TO SOME OTHER OCCUPATION (A) DO NOT SCORE AS HIGH IN PHYSICIAN INTEREST AS STUDENTS WHO DO NOT CHANGE AND (B) SCORE HIGHER IN THEIR SECOND OCCUPATION THAN IN MEDICINE

There were 139 students who said they were planning to enter medicine at the time of the first test and 531 who had another occupational plan. The former averaged 47.3 on the physician scale in contrast to 28.6 for the latter. (We have included here a number of cases not considered in Table I, for whom we have no data except that of the first test. We have learned from several sources that they became physicians; those still alive are listed in the American Medical Association Directory of 1950.)

Of the 139 students, 127 continued in medicine and 12 changed to another occupation. Five of the 12 students who changed to some other occupation were freshmen and 7 were seniors. None of the graduate students have changed their occupation from physician to nonphysician, or vice versa. After many years of practice 1 of the 12 has ceased to practice and is now dean of a school of public health; 2 were unable to finish medical school, of whom 1 is a dental technician and 1 a sanitarian; 1 is a psychologist and another a chemist; these 5 are engaged in occupations which correlate highly with medicine. The remaining 7 are engaged in a wide variety of work.

The five freshmen who changed to a nonphysician career averaged 45.4 on the physician scale in 1930, slightly higher than the 29 freshmen who continued in medicine, i.e., 43.7. The 7 seniors who left medicine, on the other hand, averaged considerably lower than the 20 who continued in medicine, i.e., 41.7 versus 48.5. Averaging the two sets of data we have mean scores of 43.2 for those who changed their occupation and 45.6 for those who did not change. Our thesis that those who choose a medical career and subsequently change to some other occupation do not score as high in physician interest as those who do not change is supported by all the available cases, although the difference is not statistically significant.

There is one clear-cut difference between the two groups—those who change from medicine score only 34.2 in 1949 while those who continue to practice medicine average 47.4.

Only 7 of the 12 men who changed to nonmedicine have entered occupations for which there are available scales. These men averaged 42.4 on this future occupation while in college in contrast to 40.5 on the physician scale. In 1949 they averaged 45.6 in their occupation and only 34.6 in physician interest. As far as the few cases go it is true that men who choose medicine and later enter another occupation score slightly higher while in college on their future occupation than medicine and score distinctly higher on their future occupation than medicine in 1949.

The men who do not change their occupations score higher on their respective occupations than the men who do change. This, we have already pointed out, is true of the cases in this study and it is also true of many other nonmedical cases (2). Apparently men who change their occupation in college or later on do not have as strong interests as those who do not change.

PROPOSITION 4: STUDENTS WHO CHOOSE A NONMEDICAL CAREER AND SUBSEQUENTLY CHANGE TO MEDICINE (A) DO NOT SCORE AS HIGH IN THE NONMEDICAL INTERESTS AS STUDENTS WHO CONTINUE THEREIN AND (B) SCORE HIGHER WHILE IN COLLEGE IN MEDICINE THAN IN THE OCCUPATION OF THEIR FIRST CHOICE

There were only two freshmen and two seniors who did not plan to enter medicine while in college and later on became physicians. The four were all considering a business career.

The physician interest scores of the four students who changed from business to medicine are given—so far as we have them—in the third line of Table VII. The data are too few to be significant.

TABLE VII. EFFECT OF CHANGING OCCUPATION UPON
PHYSICIAN INTEREST SCORES

Choice in College	Occupation in 1949	Tested in College		Retested 10–12 years later		Retested 19–22 years later	
		N	Mean	N	Mean	N	Mean
Physician	Physician	127	47.6	92	51.8	92	49.2
Don't know	Physician	5	49.8	4	54.2	4	44.2
Nonphysician	Physician	4	38.0	2	49.0	3	50.7
Physician	Nonphysician	12	43.2	8	38.2	10	34.2

Not knowing what phase of business they had in mind it is impossible to score them for their early occupational choice. No answer can be made from the data as to whether the proposition is sustained or not.

Table VII very briefly summarizes the data given in this section.

There is very little change in mean score of those who planned to be physicians while in college and are so in 1949. The data in the first line of the table indicate a rise in score of 4.2 ten to twelve years later than while in college with a drop of 2.6 in score over the next ten to twelve years. The men who said they did not know what they were going to do but entered medicine shortly afterwards score about the same as those who were sure they were going to be physicians.

As far as the data go those who changed from business to medicine scored much higher in medicine after they changed their minds than before and conversely those who changed from medicine to nonmedicine scored much higher in medicine before they changed their minds than after. But the cases are too few to draw anything but a tentative conclusion from them.

CONCLUSION

1. The higher the physician interest score while in college, the greater the chance that the student will become a physician. For an A rating the chances are 53 in 100.

2. The higher the physician interest score while in college, the greater the chance that the student will become a physician or enter an occupation related to medicine. Relatively few men with high physician interest enter an occupation which does not correlate highly with medicine and relatively few men with low physician interest enter medicine or a related occupation.

3. Students who become physicians score 96 per cent as high while in college as the criterion group. Students who do not become physicians score 56 per cent as high as the criterion group—the majority of those scoring above 56 per cent having entered an occupation which correlates highly with physician interest.

4. Students who change their occupation do not score as high as students who continue in their occupation. Apparently the former do not have as strong occupational interests as the latter.

5. Too few cases are at hand to determine the effect of changing one's occupation upon occupation scores before and after the change.

REFERENCES

1. STRONG, E. K., JR.: *Vocational Interests of Men and Women.* Stanford: Stanford University Press, 1943.
2. STRONG, E. K., JR.: "Interest scores while in college of occupations engaged in 20 years later." *Educ. & Psychol. Meas.* (in press).

8

A Tool for Selection That
Has Stood the Test of Time

Marion A. Bills

Assistant Secretary

Ætna Life Affiliated Companies

One of the tests that had its origin and at least partial development at the Bureau of Personnel Research at Carnegie Institute of Technology was the blank which has since become widely known as the Strong's Vocational Interest Test.

Because of previous experience with the predictive value of the life insurance salesman's score for both permanency of service and production with insurance salesmen, the Life Agency Department of the Ætna Life Affiliated Companies decided in the late fall of 1946 to require all persons being considered for the position of full-time agents to submit one of these blanks.

Since January 1, 1947, approximately 9400 interest blanks have been submitted to the Home Office and scored. These blanks are machine scored for 19 occupations. The scores are reported to the

General Agent who is the person in immediate contact with the prospect and have been used as one of the aids in selection. Approximately one out of ten of those tested are contracted.

For all of the persons contracted, the production is reported each three months. We therefore had in August, 1950, when this study was made, two years' complete production information on 376 men contracted between January 1, 1947, and July 1, 1948, and one year's complete production information on 277 men contracted between July 1, 1948, and July 1, 1949. As it developed, the years of 1947, 1948, and 1949 were most fortunate for an extensive investigation since these were draft-free years and any period when men are being drafted into the Armed Services complicates the setting up of a criterion which even partially depends upon permanency of service.

These two groups were first studied separately each against two criteria of success, permanency of service and production. The following tables give these results. The scores indicated on Strong's Vocational Interest Test are for life insurance selling.

TABLE I. SCORE ON STRONG'S VOCATIONAL INTEREST TEST VS.
PRODUCTION DURING TWO YEARS' EMPLOYMENT
(Men Contracted 1-1-47 to 7-1-48)

Score on Strong Interest Test	Number Contracted	Producing 60,000 First 6 mos.		Producing 120,000 First Year		Producing 2nd Year				Became Agency Assistants	
						200,000 and over		120,000– 199,999			
		No.	%	No.	%	No.	%	No.	%	No.	%
A	228	101	44.5	101	44.5	51	22.5	32	14.2	10	4.4
B+	72	16	22.2	18	25.0	6	8.4	9	12.4	1	1.4
B, B−, C	76	6	7.9	5	6.6	3	3.9	4	5.3	0	0

From Table I we see that of the persons scoring A, 41.1 per cent remained two years and produced at least 120,000 in their second year, or were made agency assistants; of those scoring B +, 22.2 per cent; and of those scoring B, B —, or C only 9.2 per cent. That is, approximately four times as large a percentage of the men scoring A might be considered successful as of those scoring B, B —, or C.

Table II gives the median production of the group remaining different periods of time.

TABLE II. SCORES ON STRONG'S VOCATIONAL INTEREST TEST VS.
PRODUCTION OF THOSE REMAINING ONE AND TWO YEARS
(Men Contracted 1-1-47 to 7-1-48)

Score on Strong Interest Test	Number Contracted	*Remaining 1 year*		Median 1st year production of those remaining at least 1 year	*Remaining 2 years*		Median 2nd year production of those remaining at least 2 years
		No.	%		No.	%	
A	228	152	66.5	155,414	97	42.5	206,680
B+	72	42	59.1	112,839	23	32.4	144,446
B, B—, C	76	26	34.2	73,814	12	15.8	133,039

From this table, we see that not only did the men scoring A tend to stay longer, but also those who stayed tended to produce more. Or, to express these tables in another way, had we contracted 18 more men scoring A instead of the 76 who scored B, B —, or C, our second year production would have been approximately the same.

You will note that the same type of relationship holds between the men scoring A, B+, and B, B —, or C in Table III as in Table I. A slightly larger percentage of the A and B+ men produced over 60,000 and 120,000 in the respective periods than of those exposed two years while a slightly smaller percentage of the B, B —, or C did. A somewhat larger percentage of each of the three score groups remained for a full year, but the median production of those remaining in each of the three groups was slightly less, perhaps due to the larger number who stayed. However, the results from the two groups are sufficiently similar so that we felt that we could combine the two and study the entire number (653), broken down by previous experience, age, and education.

TABLE III. SCORE ON STRONG'S VOCATIONAL INTEREST TEST VS.
PRODUCTION DURING ONE YEAR'S EMPLOYMENT
(Men Contracted 7-1-48 to 7-1-49)

Score on Strong Interest Test	Number Contracted	Producing 60,000 First Six Months		Producing 120,000 First Year		Remaining 1 year		
		No.	%	No.	%	No.	%	Median Production of those Remaining
A	176	86	48.8	91	51.5	138	78.2	148,499
B+	57	19	33.4	17	29.8	44	76.8	110,003
B, B−, C	44	2	4.6	2	4.6	17	38.8	69,605

One of the questions which always arises in the contracting of life insurance agents is whether or not it is better to hire persons who have had previous experience or those who are coming into the business without previous training.

Tables IV and V show the results of these two groups of agents.

TABLE IV. PRODUCTION OF 151 EXPERIENCED AGENTS
(Contracted 1-1-47 to 8-1-49)

Score on Strong Interest Test	Number Contracted	Production 1st Year					
		200,000 and over		120,000 to 199,999		Under 120,000	
		No.	%	No.	%	No.	%
A	93	24	25.8	26	28.0	43	46.2
B+	35	2	5.7	27	20.0	26	74.3
B, B−, C	23	0	0.0	0	0.0	23	100.0

TABLE V. PRODUCTION OF 502 INEXPERIENCED AGENTS
(Contracted 1-1-47 to 8-1-49)

Score on Strong Interest Test	Number Con- tracted	Production 1st Year					
		200,000 and over		120,000 to 199,999		Under 120,000	
		No.	%	No.	%	No.	%
A	311	73	23.5	70	22.5	168	54.0
B+	94	14	14.9	13	13.8	67	71.3
B, B−, C	97	4	4.1	3	3.1	90	92.8

You will note that men with previous experience scoring A on Strong's Interest Test tended to produce better than inexperienced men, but with any other test score, less well. Perhaps this is natural, since if a man has been in a profession and still does not have the same interest as men who have been successful in that field, a more definite lack is indicated. However, I always dislike to have a study come out with zero percentages, as the one on experienced agents scoring B, B −, or C did, as I know the data will not stand up. Sometime, some man with previous experience and low score is going to be successful.

Another question which arises is connected with the age of agents to be contracted and Table VI gives the results by ages.

Table VI seems to indicate that the score on life insurance selling on Strong's Vocational Interest Test predicts approximately equally well for all ages with the exception of those age 25 and under. In this age, apparently, a score of B+ results in somewhat better production than the score of A, but both A and B+ are definitely better than a lower score.

As a matter of interest, we studied the second year production of the 79 men out of the 130 in the 25-year and younger group who had been exposed for two years, and the second year median production of this group returns to the normal prediction: A, 190,022, B+, 144,446, and C, 128,562.

TABLE VI. PRODUCTION BY AGE GROUPS
(653 Agents Contracted, 1-1-47 to 8-1-49)

Score on Strong Interest Test	Number Con-tracted	Production 1st Year						Remaining 1 Year		
		200,000 and over		120,000—199,999		Under 120,000		No.	%	Median Production 1st Year
		No.	%	No.	%	No.	%			
				AGE 25 AND UNDER						
A	80	10	12.5	11	13.8	59	73.7	49	61.3	106,617
B+	25	3	12.0	7	28.0	15	60.0	18	72.0	121,049
B, B−, C	25	1	4.0	1	4.0	23	92.0	12	48.0	72,865
				AGE 26 THROUGH 29						
A	117	38	32.4	26	22.2	53	45.4	92	78.5	164,927
B+	29	4	13.8	6	20.7	19	65.5	19	65.5	136,743
B, B−, C	28	2	7.2	0	0.0	26	92.8	7	25.0	72,872
				AGE 30 THROUGH 39						
A	165	39	23.6	44	26.6	82	49.8	116	70.4	156,021
B+	53	7	13.2	3	5.7	43	81.1	33	62.4	99,864
B, B−, C	46	0	0.0	2	4.4	44	95.6	13	28.2	63,391
				AGE 40 AND OVER						
A	42	10	23.6	15	35.7	17	40.7	33	79.0	169,310
B+	22	2	9.1	4	18.2	16	32.7	16	72.5	91,195
B, B−, C	21	1	4.7	0	0.0	20	95.3	11	52.2	69,605

Another item of interest is whether there is a relation between education and success in the selling of life insurance.

A study of Table VII shows the same results as we have arrived at previously. College graduates tend to produce somewhat better than high school graduates and definitely better than those who attended college but did not graduate.

TABLE VII. PRODUCTION BY PREVIOUS EDUCATION

Score on Strong Interest Test	Number Contracted	Production 1st Year						Remaining 1 Year		
		200,000 and over		120,000— 199,999		Under 120,000		No.	%	Median Production 1st Year
		No.	%	No.	%	No.	%			
COLLEGE GRADUATES										
A	189	59	31.2	38	20.1	92	48.7	143	75.7	162,935
B+	40	8	20.0	8	20.0	24	60.0	30	75.0	121,049
B, B−, C	47	2	4.3	2	4.3	43	91.4	20	42.6	79,706
SOME COLLEGE										
A	104	14	13.5	30	28.8	60	57.7	71	68.3	136,743
B+	43	5	11.6	8	18.6	30	69.8	32	74.4	107,938
B, B−, C	26	1	3.8	1	3.8	24	92.4	8	30.8	95,204
HIGH SCHOOL GRADUATES										
A	111	24	21.6	28	25.2	59	53.2	76	68.5	166,404
B+	46	3	6.5	4	8.7	39	84.8	24	52.3	93,537
B, B−, C	47	1	2.1	0	0.0	46	97.9	14	29.8	65,042

The relation between test score groups remains approximately the same.

SUMMARY

The Strong's Vocational Interest Test which had its origin and partial development at the Bureau of Personnel Research at Carnegie Institute of Technology over thirty years ago is still one of the best tools for the selection of life insurance agents that we have available. There is apparently a pattern of interest which men who are to be successful in the selling of life insurance exhibit and this pattern of interest can be measured by the scores which applicants make on the Strong's Vocational Interest Test regardless of age, past experience, or education.

9

Identification and Selection
of Teachers

Edwin A. Lee

Dean of the School of Education
University of California
Los Angeles Campus

For a period of years the public schools of America have faced a
shortage of teachers. During the Second World War the draft took
every able-bodied young man into the armed forces; high wages
and the need for workers in all phases of the civilian war effort
likewise took great numbers of women from the teaching profession into business and industry. The auxiliary services of the
Army and Navy attracted many women teachers into such organizations as the WAVES and the WACS. Some of these returned
to teaching when war ceased, but a substantial majority was lost to
the teaching profession forever. At the same time that these men
and women were being taken from the schools those who in other
times might have been recruited to teaching were being diverted to
other callings for the same reasons.

The result was tragic for the public schools. In all but a few states "emergency" teachers were enlisted to keep the schools open. Some of these teachers were satisfactory, but the vast majority were untrained, of limited competence, and in normal times unemployable. The cessation of war did not markedly change the situation. On the contrary, there ensued in the latter years of the 1940's a startling growth in the birthrate, which soon created greatly increased demands for school facilities and teachers. At the time of writing this chapter this trend (December, 1950) showed no sign of diminishing. At the same time large-scale military activities indicated that again the public schools would be competing with demands and attractions which would make the problem of recruiting adequate personnel for teaching fully as difficult as before.

Coincident with the trends just described are some favorable ones. There is a growing tendency to recognize the importance of the public school as one of the indispensable institutions of American civilization, indeed as the one upon which the successful continuance of all the others depends. Consequently the role of the teacher has been enhanced in the public mind; citizens everywhere, particularly parents, have shown an increased interest in the schools of their communities; and salaries have been increased to bring the incomes of teachers more nearly into line with professions requiring comparable training. Naturally, the most important trend which is emerging from those just mentioned is an increased attention on the part of employers and teacher-education institutions to the problems of recruiting, selecting, and promoting teachers, supervisors, and administrators for the public schools of America. It is to the general consideration of these problems that this chapter is addressed.

SOME BASIC IDEAS

From the beginning of our history as a nation education has loomed large. Nowhere has this truth been better stated than in the

Ordinance of 1787 which Congress drafted to cover the organization and government of the Northwest Territory. These are the words:

Religion, morality, and knowledge, being necessary to good government and the happiness of mankind, schools and the means of education shall forever be encouraged.

In a democracy it is of vital importance that the education of future generations be guided by wise and well-adjusted persons. This can be assured only if constant attention is given to the selection and upgrading of teachers and other educational personnel at the various stages of training and employment. Good schools rest fundamentally on good teachers—everything else is added thereunto.

When large numbers of teachers are needed to man the classrooms of our schools there is frequently a temptation to relax standards in order to meet the pressing demands of parents and citizens that there be schools for their children. "Better a poor or untrained teacher," they say, "than no classes at all." So in the great state in which this is being written, in 1950 one out of every eight persons now teaching in California public schools holds an "emergency credential," [1] a substandard document, a situation not limited to Western states. If American civilization is to be maintained and if it is to flourish, such practices must be replaced by an aggressive policy of recruiting in which the criteria of selection shall conform to high and acceptable standards.

SOME GENERAL PROPOSITIONS

There are three general propositions which have guided the writer in formulating this chapter. The first is that the problem of selection must not be considered as a single step in a process. Rather it must be viewed as a series of events beginning with the recruitment of promising youth as students of teachers colleges and schools of education, continuing throughout the training period into placement,

---

[1] STONE, J. C., and DOUGLASS, A. A.: "Teacher Supply and Demand." *California Schools*, 1950, 21:113.

and including succeeding selections for particular posts in the school system and transfer from one school to another or from teaching to supervision or administration.

The second proposition is the self-evident one that selection, whenever and wherever it occurs, must be viewed at all levels in the light of the qualities and requirements demanded by the particular positions involved.

Proposition three, almost as self-evident, is that the total configuration of characteristics of any given candidate, including education, experience, intellectual ability, knowledge of subject matter, and personality traits, must be considered in selecting a teacher for a particular position.

SOME IMPORTANT AREAS OF INFORMATION

There are at least six areas of information which should be taken into account when selecting educational personnel. No one of the six may be left out of the total file of information which should be assembled concerning every individual who purposes to serve in the public schools. Certain areas can only be filled in as the individual involved progresses through the training and early employment periods. Others are susceptible to immediate recording upon first contact with the potential teacher. Most information in the six areas will be subject to amplification and change as the experience and maturity of the candidate develop. The essential fact to remember is that the older and more experienced the individual becomes, the more complete and accurate will be the data under each of the six categories.

PERSONAL AND SOCIAL CHARACTERISTICS

The material under this category falls under four heads. There is first the general information found on almost any personnel record card, including such items as age, nationality, sex, educational history, marital status, and the like.

The second category has to do with information about the

personal adjustment of the individual concerned. Under this head the examiner would expect to find data, increasingly accurate as the file accumulates, relative to such matters as the following:

a. Presence of or freedom from conflicts, tensions, frustrations, and other emotional factors which not only contribute to unstable personality but also tend to produce undesirable effects in children.

b. Evidence of emotional stability in terms of control of personal feelings under trying situations, especially with children; and of manner in which disappointments and failures are met.

c. Evidence of confidence in self and in personal abilities.

d. Presence of enthusiasm for living and especially for children and their potentialities.

Such information is not easy to accumulate and is frequently not objective, but psychology and psychiatry are constantly enlarging the borders of our knowledge and skill in this area. Certain it is that in this realm often reside the real reasons for success or failure as a teacher.

Category three is similar to the one just discussed but involves information about the total organizational pattern of the person under scrutiny. Here we are concerned with the dominant traits of temperament which characterize the individual, the consistency of temperamental traits with each other and with reality, and whether the individual is in control of the temperament or the temperament controls the individual.

The fourth category involves information regarding relationships with other people and includes such items as these:

a. Evidence of sympathetic attitude in personal relations.

b. Evidence of enthusiastic and understanding interest in activities and problems of others, especially children, together with the desire to be of assistance.

c. Evidence of tact and poise in dealing with other persons in difficult situations.

d. The frequency with which the individual is sought for help on personal matters as well as school tasks, particularly by pupils.

INTELLECTUAL ABILITIES AND ACCOMPLISHMENTS

The second important area has to do with information concerning those characteristics which are primarily intellectual. Such data fall into at least six categories, all of which, excepting the first and that only in part, may be measured with a fair degree of reliability.

Category one includes the phenomenon of intelligence, more properly the various intelligences, appropriate to teaching, and the elusive quality described as special aptitude for teaching. Concerning the first we are not without reasonably dependable instruments for measuring the powers and abilities of human beings which may be grouped loosely under the term intelligence, but no one has succeeded very well thus far in developing a special aptitude test for teaching. Indeed no one has described accurately what constitutes special aptitude for teaching. Perhaps the increased interest in and emphasis upon teacher selection may encourage significant research in this important segment of the problem.

Number two covers much in a very brief statement. It is the ability to understand and express ideas clearly and simply. In essence all education is communication of ideas in both directions, from the teacher to the pupil and from the pupil to the teacher. Fortunately the possession or lack of this ability to communicate is easily discovered. It goes almost without saying that low ability should disqualify an individual from entering or advancing in the teaching profession.

The third category has to do with general culture, including knowledge of contemporary problems and happenings. Jacques Barzun, in his article "The Educated Man" written for *Life's* special issue on U. S. Schools (October 16, 1950), speaks of a man's culture as "The enrichment of his own mind." This is perhaps as good a definition as can be found of the characteristic with which we are here concerned. To a degree and not altogether superficially it is possible to arrive at an estimate of a man's cultural attainment, his "C. Q.," so to speak. It is of supreme importance that the children and youth of America in the decades ahead be taught by men and women of culture in its truest sense.

Next in the list are knowledge and understanding of the growth of human beings as organisms and as personalities. It is quite possible to imagine Barzun's "educated man" as completely unsophisticated in this facet of culture. It is impossible to imagine an "educated teacher" unaware of and uninterested in the phenomena of human growth and development. So we seek to evaluate attainment of understanding of human psychology.

The fifth category grows out of the two which have preceded, indeed is an extension of them. It is the power and the desire (they do not necessarily always appear together) to synthesize knowledge and experience into a meaningful composite. Perhaps one is not truly an educated man who has not achieved this synthesis at any given time. Just as truly is he not educated if at that given time he rests content in the belief that he need synthesize no more. In any case, we want more and more truly educated men and women in our schools at all levels and in all types of positions. Our selective processes should guarantee that none such shall be lost in the winnowing.

Special competence in the subject field and/or skills which the candidate expects to teach is the sixth category. To name it is to emphasize its importance and the comparative accuracy with which it can be evaluated.

PROFESSIONAL EFFECTIVENESS

This area subdivides into two sections, the one dealing mainly with professional concepts, the other with instructional techniques.

Both are susceptible to some degree of objective treatment in any process of selection.

The first has to do with the personal concept of the actual or potential teacher as to the function of education in a democratic society. It may properly be called the personal philosophy of education held by that person. Included in any consideration of this aspect of the selective process are such items as these:

a. The concept of the role of the public school in furthering the ends of a democratic civilization.

b. The concept of the role of the school in fostering a maximum development of the potentialities of each individual.

c. The concept of the part played in the educative process by person-to-person relationships—teacher to pupil, parent to child, pupil to pupil, and so on.

d. The concept of the part played by other agencies in the total education of the individual: the church, the press, radio, television, the home, the playground, the neighborhood.

Instructional skills and abilities, the second subcategory under this head, concerns those techniques which distinguish the effective from the inept teachers. In the main these techniques are observable and can sometimes be crudely measured, but essentially evaluation rests upon subjective judgment rather than objective measurement. There are seven, as follows:

a. Ability to analyze the developmental needs of the individual pupils on the basis of background, ability, temperament, and motivation.

b. Ability to plan and organize experiences with pupils.

c. Ability to guide pupils in the interpretation of experience.

d. Ability to stimulate pupils to employ a variety of effective learning techniques.

e. Ability to work with pupils in securing the highest possible levels of personal achievement compatible with their needs and abilities.

f. Ability to interpret to the parent the needs of pupils.

g. Ability to interpret to the public the purposes and procedures of the schools.

PERSONAL EXPERIENCE

The area of personal experience is, of course, almost boundless in scope and variety. Any program of teacher-selection must be limited to evaluating experiences which have a bearing upon the potential profession of the candidate. There are at least six subareas which should be included.

The first concerns the amount and kind of informal experiences with children and youth which the biography of the candidate indicates. If the picture portrays a person who appears to have played and worked with others of his age group, if there is evidence of a spirit of cooperation and give-and-take, if there are examples of assignments and acceptance of responsibility within the group, there is reason to believe that these same qualities may persist in later professional life. If as the individual matures there are instances of interest in children and youth—Sunday-school teaching, playground direction, and cub-scout leadership are examples—there is further evidence of the possession of qualities that are highly desirable in the total make-up of a teacher.

The second subarea concerns the amount and kind of extra-curricular activities in high school and college displayed by the record. Other things being equal, that person who has been a Boy or Girl Scout and later a Scout leader, or who has been a member of the "Y" during high school days and later an officer or leader of "Hi-Y" groups, exhibits characteristics which are valuable to one who expects to teach. Membership in such activities as clubs, dramatic organizations, athletic teams, especially if there are evidences of leadership based on selection by his fellows, is significant. Wherever there is evidence of interest in and guidance of younger children there is a clue of importance. Complete absence of such information warrants at least the suspicion that the individual under consideration lacks qualities which are important to success as a teacher and for which there should be elsewhere in the record factors to compensate for this.

The two subareas just discussed have to do mainly with experiences prior to professional training and are therefore most pertinent to the selection of candidates for initial training. The three that follow concern experiences involved in actual teaching.

Perhaps the set of experiences of most significance in the selection of individuals for the profession of teaching is that which falls in the subarea of supervised or cadet teaching. Here for the first time under more or less controlled conditions the potential teacher tries out and is tried in the class room. Here all his previous education, general and professional, his personality, poise, and inventiveness are tried in the crucible of actual teaching. Here is the testing point: success within reasonable limits guarantees a career in education; failure means denial of the privilege of teaching. It follows that evaluation of performance must aim to be accurate, objective, and clearly evident to all who have occasion to use the data, including the candidate who is being evaluated.

Selection after basic professional training has been completed is in terms of appointment to or promotion within a given system. The fourth subarea, therefore, is concerned with the amount and kind of regular teaching experience. The criteria involved in selection are not radically different from those applicable to supervised teaching, the difference being mainly in procedural technique rather than kind. There is more time to make the evaluation; there is less at stake for the candidate, particularly after the probationary period has been passed. There comes a time, frequently soon, when the evaluation is no longer selective in nature, rather it is confirmatory— Mr. A. or Miss B. is simply a "superior teacher," nothing can be added.

The fifth and sixth subareas must therefore be in terms of activities other than teaching. Number five involves the nature and degree of participation in professional activities outside the classroom. Included are such responsibilities as committee work—in the school system, in professional organizations of teachers, on regional or state or national commissions; administrative assignments—in the school system, as officers in local or state or national professional organizations; authorship—of reports, textbooks, surveys, special research projects, and the like. It is from the ranks of teachers, supervisors, and administrators whose biographies include such data that selections for promotion and advancement are made.

The fifth body of information to be included in this section concerns the amount and kind of activities outside the field of education, embracing on the one hand work other than teaching and administration, and on the other service and responsibility in the community at large. In the first fall such experiences as military service, summer occupations, occupations followed prior to entering teaching, in fact any activity other than teaching to which a man or woman has given a reasonable period of time either for pay or personal satisfaction. In the second are included services in such activities as community chests, playground and park commissions, hospital boards, library committees, city-planning commissions, church boards, committees on fiestas or pageants or 4th-of-July celebrations—the list is almost endless. In its detail and its scope reside data taken into account by Boards of Education when they are selecting teachers and administrators for the systems under their charge.

That any of the five subareas enumerated lend themselves to precise and objective treatment is not claimed. Nevertheless, to the degree that the various data suggested can be assembled accurately, organized in such a fashion that they can be compared with similar data, and the interpretation of their meaning deduced by the application of common sense, to that degree can such material be used as significant indices in the total problem of selection of teacher personnel.

PROFESSIONAL GROWTH

The author includes this section with some want of confidence. None of the information suggested below constitutes truly objective evidence. Most of the questions can only be answered yes or no, and those that lend themselves to quantitative responses will only elicit numbers which are meaningless in themselves. Nevertheless, affirmative answers are significant in that they point to evidences of that personal growth in the individual which generally indicates the possession of a spirit and morale truly professional in nature. Certainly negative responses would give reason to suspect little if any professional drive. In any case, boards and superintendents seeking capable personnel for their schools want to know answers to such questions and they tend for obvious reasons to favor those whose record presents affirmative rather than negative responses. The odds are all in favor of the affirmative.

The material is presented under three heads, in question form, and without comment.

a. Is there evidence of professional interest in terms of—
1. Initiative displayed in planning new and more effective ways of teaching?
2. Amount and kind of postgraduate and summer session study?
3. Amount and kind of professional reading?
4. Amount and kind of attendance and participation in meetings of professional societies?

b. Is there evidence of a positive attitude toward professional responsibilities in terms of—
1. Acceptance of responsibility for aiding pupils to develop their potentialities?
2. Initiative, independence, and originality?
3. Completing assigned responsibilities with little supervision and minimum digression?
4. Willingness to make decisions on the basis of available

information and to alter decisions when additional information becomes available?

c. Is there evidence of positive attitudes and habits of thinking in terms of—

1. Tolerance for points of view and patterns of thinking which are not in complete harmony with own position?
2. Intellectual and professional curiosity?
3. Alertness in utilizing research findings?
4. Critical and scientific attitude toward the instructional field and educational problems?

HEALTH AND PHYSICAL FITNESS

The area of health and physical fitness would seem to be of all areas with which we are concerned in this chapter the simplest for which to devise selective measures and devices. Most states require a doctor's certificate of health and physical fitness for certification to teach in the public schools. Likewise practically all cities of any size impose their own medical examinations as a condition of employment. The institution with which the author is associated requires approval of the medical officer of the University before permission to enroll for supervised teaching, a practice followed by all of the better professional schools and colleges of education. The bases on which these approvals are given are most general in definition: acceptable physical and mental health, freedom from certain physical defects or abnormalities, and absence of apparent susceptibility to certain functional disorders. Generally any licensed physician may make and sign the report of examination which the State certificating authority requires, and generally the physician states that *in his judgment* the health of the applicant is such that he should or should not be granted the credential he seeks.

Thus in a most fundamental aspect of the selective process whether or not an individual shall be permitted to teach in the public schools rests upon the judgment of persons who rarely are intimately

Name.....................................Date of birth..........

Weight..............Height...............Skin.................

Deformities................ Posture............Joints..............

Speech defects...

Eyes..............Acuity: R.....L.....Corrected to: R.....L.....

Ears........Hearing (Audiometer 4A) R....L....Tone R....L....

Nose and sinuses...

Throat.............Tonsils present........... Diseased...........

Breath..............Teeth................ Gums................

Heart...

Lungs...

Evidence of tuberculosis.......................................

Blood pressure S..............D..............Pulse rate..........

Abdomen...........................Hernia...................

Genitourinary...

Endocrine system....................Nutrition.................

Nervous system...

Does the applicant present any evidence of mental or emotional instability?...

Special laboratory findings, when found necessary for diagnostic purposes: albuminaria, glycosuria, blood tests, G. C., Wassermann......
....

I HEREBY CERTIFY That the foregoing is a full, true and
correct report of an examination of the person named therein, conducted by me on the day of the date hereof. I hereby further certify
that in my opinion, based on such examination, the health of the

applicant is such that he
{
should be granted the credential...
should not be granted the
credential ...

check one

Date........ (SIGNATURE OF PHYSICIAN)...................

Name of physician (type or print)...........California license no....

Address of physician...

Institution/Department for whom examination is conducted.........

acquainted with educational requirements, who frequently are swayed by personal considerations, and who generally handle the whole problem in a most casual fashion.

There is reproduced above the form for Health Examinations required in the State of California.[2]

The physician filling out this form finds on the reverse of the blank a list of physical defects any of which "may be considered sufficient reason for denying a candidate a credential." This list includes such items as:

> Gross unsightly blemishes including severe acne.
> Pathological overweight.
> Impediment of speech.
> Neglected carious teeth.
> Organic heart disease.
> Pulmonary tuberculosis.
> Chronic recurrent appendicitis.
> Epilepsy.
> History or evidence of emotional or mental instability.

Altogether there are 42 of these items catalogued under 15 heads. The physician *may* determine the importance of any item in approving or disapproving an application. If he approves his judgment is final; if he disapproves the applicant may appeal to the State Board of Education.

It would appear that far from being simple this phase of the selective process is complicated and baffling, particularly in the area of mental and emotional stability. We need thorough and dependable research involving thousands of cases and covering long periods of time before we can speak with assurance concerning improvement in the present procedure. We can be certain, however, that the need for improvement is imperative.

---

[2] California State Department of Education: "Regulations Relating to Credentials for Public School Service." *Bulletin of California State Department of Education,* 1946, *16:* 100.

SOME SELECTIVE PRACTICES

The preceding sections have dealt with general and theoretical aspects of the problem of selection. This section will report certain practices indicative of trends which appear to be developing. There is a considerable literature on the subject, much of which is disappointing, due mainly to a failure to follow through on projects which initially gave promise of contributing significantly.

Three segments of the problem will be treated briefly: Selection of Individuals for Professional Education; Selection of Individuals for Employment; and Selection of Individuals for Promotion or Salary Increase.

SELECTION OF INDIVIDUALS FOR PROFESSIONAL EDUCATION

The first episodes in the selective process have to do with the problem of choosing from the youth interested in teaching those who should be encouraged to undertake professional training. What practices have been found useful? What criteria can be depended upon for guidance and selection?

Ruth G. Boynton in 1946, in an unpublished master's thesis,[3] reviewed and synthesized "the literature pertaining to the personal and preprofessional qualifications which may be predictive of success in teaching." Boynton chose twelve qualities of teachers and on the basis of wide reading from a voluminous bibliography grouped them under three main categories:

. . . (1) those which are basic and essential to all teachers but which do not ordinarily serve to distinguish between successful and unsuccessful teachers because of the homogeneity of the teaching group in these qualities; (2) those which seem to give promise of distinguishing between the successful and unsuccessful teachers and teacher candidates; and (3) those which appear to be desirable attributes in a teacher, but

---

[3] BOYNTON, RUTH G. "The Selection of Students Preparing for Teaching." Unpublished master's thesis, Los Angeles, University of California, 1946.

about which insufficient data were found to establish them either as basic requirements or as factors for distinguishing potential success.

The following division [4] seems justified by the reports studied:

1. Qualifications essential for all teachers:

   Intelligence—average for college students

   Scholastic achievement—average for college students or high enough to meet any special requirements which have been established

   Health—good physical and mental health and freedom from disabling defects

2. Qualifications which may distinguish between successful and unsuccessful teachers:

   Interest—a primary interest in educational processes and in children

   Motivation—a vital purpose derived from understanding the value of education rather than one based on extraneous factors

   Personality—Desirable traits: the presence of a reasonable number of the traits found to be assets, coupled with few or none of the traits associated with poor teachers. Adequate personal and social adjustment

3. Qualifications which may be necessary or desirable but about which insufficient objective evidence was found:

   Speech, reading, and writing skill

   Special skills in music, art, mechanics, and the like

   Democratic social attitudes

   Breadth of interest

   Breadth of experience

The careful reader will discern that only eleven qualities appear in this listing. The twelfth was "aptitude for teaching." Boynton discovered no measures for determining teaching aptitude. Of those tests bearing titles which suggested they were instruments for

---

[4] *Ibid.*, p. 100, 101.

determining an individual's over-all aptitude for teaching she wisely concludes "that they are tests of some aspect of personality, of professional information, or for academic and cultural achievement, and that they should be used only in conjunction with other measures." [5]

The general impression one gains from reading Boynton's study is that despite many promising starts in the direction of dependable objective measuring devices there has been little advance. For measuring verbal intelligence she suggests the Psychological Examination of the American Council on Education and the Ohio State Psychological Examination, but she finds no decisive evidence of relationship between intelligence and potential teaching ability, except within broad limits. She discovers no better criterion of academic achievement than high school and college grades. Physical and psychiatric examinations she leaves to the physicians. She finds no interest inventory reliable, and she is skeptical of the value of personality ratings, although "In the field of personality adjustment and mental hygiene the Thurstone (Emotionality) Schedule or possibly the Bell or Bernreuter, using the Flanagan scales, may be useful." [6]

One thing is quite clear from Boynton's investigation: there is urgent need for sound protracted research concerning ways and means of recruiting and selecting youth for the teaching profession. There are some reasonably good tools available. There is the know-how to develop other tools. All that seems to be lacking is the will and the finances to enter into the complicated and time-consuming processes which will be required.

One other reference should be quoted: the *Standards for Student Personnel Services and Evaluative Criteria* recently devised as a part of the accreditation procedure of the American Association of

[5] *Ibid.*, p. 83.
[6] *Ibid.*, p. 103.

Colleges for Teacher Education. Relative to selection of students for teacher education is the following:

PROGRESSIVE SELECTION AND RETENTION

Progressive selection and vocational orientation of students should be practiced from the first term onward, through the application of standards of scholarship, personality, health, and behavior established for continuation and promotion. Through a selective process, the student should be admitted to candidacy for teacher preparation. It is recommended that the techniques of selection should include consideration of: (1) the quality of the applicant's scholarship; (2) recommendations or descriptive statements from counselors and other staff members relative to the candidate's personal and social fitness to become a teacher; (3) indications of qualities of leadership, cooperation, responsibility, and general citizenship by participation in extra-course activities; (4) status and achievement in health; (5) standing in college testing program; (6) voice, speech, and oral and written English records; and (7) evidence of ability to understand children and to work with them.

SELECTION OF INDIVIDUALS FOR EMPLOYMENT

The selection of individuals for employment ranges all the way from the procedure in which an all-wise superintendent or principal chooses on the basis of a fifteen-minute interview and "playing his hunch," to the highly complicated program of examinations and interviewing followed by the large school systems. The disturbing fact is that not infrequently the man who plays his hunches secures just as promising and competent teachers as are chosen by the more involved and costly method, particularly if he supplements his interview by examination of the record of the candidates.

In general the acceptable procedure includes the following:

a. An application form setting forth training and experience of the candidate, often rather fully.

b. Reference material concerning the candidate, either on a rating scale, or in terms of personal letters, or both.

c. Transcripts of record in schools and colleges.
d. Record of performance in the National Teachers Examination.
e. Record of performance in supplementary examinations administered by the school department; including special fields, such as music or agriculture or art.
f. An interview, generally with an interviewing committee which may use a form such as the *Bingham Rating Form for the Use of Interviewers and Examiners.*
g. The determination of a "score" based upon the evaluation of training, experience, test results, and the interview, all weighted in terms of preferred and less-preferred values and permitting a maximum possible score generally of 100 or 500 or 1000 points.
h. The establishment of an eligibility list in terms of total score achieved, with a certain favorable weighting sometimes given to "home-talent," and almost always given to individuals with war-service records.

It will be noted that some of the items named above can be treated with a reasonable degree of objectivity. Thus the use of the Bingham Rating Form permits the interview to be scored. The scores of the National Teachers Examination are highly accurate and can be compared with national norms. The total score accordingly has better meaning and more dependability than it otherwise would have.

It follows, in a community which has adopted such a scheme of selection, that when appointments are to be made the superintendent will be expected to recommend the name or names at the top of the list. Nothing so guarantees the integrity of a School Board or a superintendent as the general knowledge that eligibility lists are determined fairly and objectively and adhered to in making appointments. And nothing reduces the political pressure to the vanishing point so effectively.

The difference between procedure in selecting experienced and inexperienced teachers is, of course, in degree rather than kind. More emphasis is placed on teaching performance, less on collegiate record; more on judgments of previous employers, less upon judgment of supervisors of practice teaching. Each of the eight items, however, is taken into account for its full value in terms of the situation in which the selections are involved.

Probably at no place in the complete process of selection are the results more dependable and satisfying than here, yet the opportunities for significant research and consequent improvement are many and challenging.

SELECTION OF INDIVIDUALS FOR PROMOTION OR SALARY INCREASE

What has been written in the preceding section applies with even more force to the selection of individuals for promotion within a school system. The way to the top for individuals of ability and professional drive must always be open and the procedures by which promotions are determined must always be above suspicion. Evidences of performance become increasingly important as teachers or administrators become more mature. Examinations and interviews supplement and confirm what the record of experience suggests, but they do not overweigh proven successful experience. The problem is simplified by the fact that the number of candidates involved at a given time is far less than those seeking a teaching appointment; at the same time it is complicated by the maturity of the candidates and the importance of the posts to which promotion is sought. Therefore the examinations have to be more carefully prepared and graded, the interview has to be much more skillfully conducted and evaluated, the reference material more intelligently scrutinized and interpreted. Mistakes at these levels are more costly, harder to rectify, and the after-effects more difficult to eradicate. Here, too, there is need for careful and subtle research.

Selection of individuals for salary increase is a slightly different matter. Most forward-looking communities have salary schedules which provide automatic increases with the passage of time. This is an easy way to reward persistence but it provides no incentive for self-improvement. Increasingly, therefore, provision is being made for recognition of service beyond the call of duty. This sometimes takes the negative form of no increase after a given period has elapsed unless there be evidence of professional growth; or it may be positive in that an additional increase is provided if there be satisfactory evidence of growth.

The most interesting development in this area is the 1947 New York State minimum salary law, the essential provision of which was discussed by Morrison as follows: [7]

School authorities shall pay each teacher the minimum salary herein required together with the annual increments represented by his years of service in the school district until the teacher has completed six years of service. Such increments shall be known as automatic increments. The balance of the increments for which teachers may become eligible after additional years of service shall be known as promotional increments; except that a teacher who is granted a promotional increment at the end of the sixth year of service shall be entitled to two further annual automatic increments. Each teacher shall have opportunities to qualify for promotional increments through satisfactory teaching service and in addition, objective evidence of one or more of the following special contributions:

a. Exceptional service to the pupils for whom the teacher is individually responsible, such as unusually skillful or stimulating classroom work, personal contacts with pupils or assistance to pupils in out-of-school activities.

b. Exceptional service to the community through non-school activities directly related to the interests and well-being of young people (not necessarily the teacher's own pupils), in such matters as the prevention of juvenile delinquency or the provision of opportunities for recreation.

c. Substantial increase in the value of service rendered to pupils

---

[7] MORRISON, J. C.: "Implementation of the Promotional Increment Provision of the New York State Teachers Salary Law." Unpublished address given at Atlantic City Conference on Selection of Teachers, February 25, 1948, pp. 1, 2. Our italics.

through the teacher's participation in non-school activities, such as summer-time work related to the teacher's field of instruction of social service projects, for which the teacher is not otherwise compensated or is only nominally compensated.

d. Substantial increase in the value of service rendered to pupils, as a result of education beyond the level of the master's degree, education not formally credited toward a degree, or continued approved study by teachers who do not hold a college degree.

Based upon these standards, *and with participation by classroom teachers in the formulation, application, and review of such standards in accordance with regulations established by the commissioner of education,* school authorities shall adopt bylaws governing the granting of promotional increments.

The purposes of this Law run deeper than merely relating salary to competence. At this point, some fundamental concepts may be noted. (1) The concept back of the automatic increments is that the teacher who is worth retaining should be guaranteed an income sufficient to maintain a reasonable cultural and professional status. We think the sixth step on the New York schedule is not sufficient to meet this test. (2) The end of the automatic increments should come early enough in the teacher's career so that he can transfer to another field of work if he finds that he and teaching are not particularly suited to each other. (3) The chief reason for promotional increments is to improve teacher growth and teaching service. Therefore, they should begin relatively early. They should be so administered that the door will be always open for advancement. (4) Basing promotion on exceptional service is not so revolutionary as it may seem at first thought. Most of the states have tenure laws with a probationary period. In New York, at the end of the probationary period the superintendent must recommend in writing the renewal of the teacher's appointment. A negative judgment at this point in the teacher's career is much more serious than any negative judgment will be in administering the promotional increments, for in the latter case the teacher's tenure is not affected. Also, the administration of the promotional increment is not essentially different in principle from the promotion of a teacher to the rank of principal or supervisor.

The fundamental issue in New York is whether teachers will accept the opportunity and the responsibility given them by the Law to participate in the "formulation, application and review" of the standards by which they shall be judged. Acceptance of this responsibility will go far toward giving teaching a high rating among the professions.[8]

CONCLUSION

The problem of selection of personnel has always faced employers whether the payroll is small or large, but the "hiring and firing" of employees until recent decades has been almost completely unscientific both in specifications of jobs to be filled and methods of filling them. A foreman hired a man because he liked "the cut of his jib," office managers selected clerical workers and typists in terms of color of hair and shape of chin. Some forward-looking employers, including school boards, at the turn of the century, were attempting to select upon the basis of written examinations, but such were neither skillfully prepared nor accurately evaluated. They were better than snap judgments, but not much.

When institutions such as the Division of Applied Psychology at Carnegie Institute of Technology began their pioneer work in developing dependable methods and criteria of selection a new profession, the personnel worker, commenced to assume stature and significance. Today, not quite a half-century later, no industrial or commercial establishment of any size or consequence is without its "division of personnel," in fact none could function long or effectively lacking such a division. The public schools, which in total in any community rank at the top in numbers employed, have been profoundly affected by this extraordinary development in the field of applied psychology. When used appropriately and with understanding, tests of intelligence, ability, achievement, mechanical and clerical aptitudes, interest inventories, rating scales have all contributed significantly to the securing of better educated and more

---

[8] *Ibid.*, pp. 13, 14.

suitable personnel in the various levels and varieties of educational service.

No one who is at all sophisticated concerning the problem of teacher recruitment and selection, however, is satisfied with the progress made thus far. The most significant research still remains to be prosecuted. We know too little of what constitutes good teaching, of what it takes in terms of personal equipment to succeed in what is after all one of the most complex and baffling of professions. It is comparatively simple to select a competent stenographer; it is not nearly so simple to select a competent teacher of shorthand. And it is extremely difficult to select a potentially successful teacher of any subject or field from youth who have not yet chosen a field of occupational endeavor. Despite the pressures which teacher-shortage will impose upon professional schools of education in the decades between 1950 and 1970, in fact because of them, the need for the development of more dependable scientific programs of selection based upon accurate and imaginative research presents a challenge which cannot be refused. It is in this area that educators and psychologists working together may make some of their most significant contributions in the years ahead.

10

Professional Use of the Clinical Method in Employee Selection

Glen U. Cleeton

Dean, Division of Humanistic and Social Studies
Carnegie Institute of Technology
Pittsburgh, Pennsylvania

In the early application of psychology to employment problems, the clinical method was the basic procedure used. Primarily, an effort was made to determine the characteristics of the job and to specify the qualities or traits of the person most likely to perform the job satisfactorily. Depending upon the professional skill and ingenuity of the psychologist attempting to analyze the problem, the manner of determining job requirements and probable qualifications varied considerably.

Often the mental set of the psychologist, that is, his basic philosophy or the school of psychology to which he belonged, influenced his judgment in detailing specifications of qualifications. Because of lack of familiarity with employment situations, many naive assumptions were made about the requirements of jobs performed by office, store, factory, and transportation workers. Furthermore, because of lack of adequate measuring instruments and almost complete absence of standards, appraisals made, although logical in terms of academic psychology, were frequently speculative and superficial from a work-operation point of view. Consequently, selection procedures, even though based on laboratory techniques commonly used by experimental psychologists of the period, were applied without proper regard being given to concepts of reliability and validity.

Although confronted with almost insurmountable limitations, much valuable pioneering and exploratory work in employee selection was done by a few American and European psychologists prior to the First World War.[1] Shortly thereafter more definitive applications of psychology to problems of employee selection, classification, and placement were attempted by several groups of psychologists. Probably the most concentrated effort anywhere in the world to apply psychology to the solution of these problems was made by a group operating as the Division of Applied Psychology at the Carnegie Institute of Technology from 1915 to 1924. The work of this group, under the initial direction of Dr. Walter Dill Scott and later Dr. Walter V. Bingham, made possible the formulation of many of the most important principles and procedures now widely used in employee selection. Adapting statistical methods to the treatment of psychological data, particular emphasis was placed on questions of reliability and validity, test construction, and the determination of norms or standards, but at no time did this group overlook the fact that human diagnosis, classification, and placement

---

[1] A brief chronology of early events in the establishment of industrial psychology as a new field is presented in Bruce V. Moore and George W. Hartmann, *Readings in Industrial Psychology*. New York: Appleton-Century-Crofts, Inc., 1931, pp. 3–8.

are broad problems which cannot be solved by mere interpretation of a few test scores or other limited quantitative evidence.[2]

Despite the significant work done by the Carnegie group, which demonstrated the importance of clinical procedures in employee selection, many employment psychologists continue to place disproportionate emphasis on normative interpretations of data obtained through the administration of psychological tests to the exclusion of the clinical analysis of test results and quantitative and qualitative information made available through other means. In fact, a considerable amount of the literature on employee selection seeks to impart special virtues to psychological tests by emphasizing the subjectivity of the interview, and the limitations of traditional tools of selection such as letters of application, personal history records, application forms, letters of recommendation, and reports of former employers or others acquainted with the candidate for employment.

The fact that psychological tests usually are found to have higher statistical reliability than other sources of information has caused many psychologists to dismiss as not subject to critical analysis and evaluation information other than that obtained through the administration of standardized psychological measuring devices. This emphasis is frequently so insistent that the importance of professional judgment is overlooked. Instead of the psychologist being the master and his tools or measuring devices being his servant, the instruments of measurement become the master and the psychologist the servant.[3]

Many industrial psychologists worship with such intense faith at

---

[2] This viewpoint is clearly implied in Walter V. Bingham and Max Freyd, *Procedures in Employment Psychology*. New York: McGraw-Hill, 1926. For a brief statement of the formation and development of the Division of Applied Psychology at Carnegie see Arthur W. Tarbell, *The Story of Carnegie Tech, 1900 to 1935.* New York: Carnegie Press, 1937, pp. 60–65.

[3] A businessman's appraisal of the merits of professional judgment in the application of psychology to the selection of employees, especially at the management level, is presented in an article entitled, "Psychologists in business." *Forbes Magazine,* 1950, *66:* 12–13.

the shrines of laboratory and statistical techniques that they either assume the role of a technician laying claim to a body of specialized knowledge or, with the false modesty of the pure scientist, deny the existence of capacity to evaluate, diagnose, or prescribe as a professional psychologist. These attitudes were so prevalent among psychologists in the formative stages of applied psychology that it was not uncommon practice for business firms to purchase psychological tests and have them administered and interpreted by an office clerk or personnel interviewer, or for "quacks" to seize upon opportunities to sell "psychological services" to employers. Thus, by failing to emphasize the importance of professional knowledge and skill in evaluation, the psychologist indirectly encouraged what might be termed the "patent-medicine" or "trust-buy-and-try" era in the use of psychology in employee selection. To some extent, patent-medicine applications of psychological instruments still survive.

One of the difficulties encountered in the application of psychology to employee selection is the seeming reluctance of psychologists to admit that the development of measuring devices and their statistical validation is a problem distinctly apart from the problem of using such devices to obtain information necessary for the formulation of professional judgment. As a consequence the applied psychologist often strives to create and apply fundamental knowledge at one and the same time.[4] This conflict might be resolved by a clearer recognition that the problems involved in the development and validation of psychological measuring devices are similar to the problems dealt with by research scientists, whereas the problems involved in the application of these devices are similar to those of the engineer or medical practitioner.

Both the engineer and medical practitioner use fundamental

---

[4] This problem is treated in a chapter entitled, "Research and judgment in work relations" in Glen U. Cleeton, *Making Work Human*. Antioch Press, 1949, pp. 260-280. See also Walter V. Bingham, "On the possibility of an applied psychology." *Psychological Review*, 1923, *30*: 289-298.

knowledge of basic principles, apply devices for making diagnoses and interpretations, compare with established standards the results of tests or other indicators, and then decide on a plan of action. In this respect the art and practice of the applied psychologist resemble that of the engineer and the physician. Admittedly the engineer, the physician, and the psychologist will not perform professionally in precisely the same manner, yet it must be clear to anyone familiar with professional practice in these fields that the problems encountered require a similar approach. Even though the professional style of each may differ, there is much in common in the methods of thought involved. Hence, it may be assumed that the psychologist will attain professional status through the use of clinical methods to the same extent that these methods are used by the engineer and physician.[5]

The *clinical* approach to the solution of any problem involves both *analysis* and *synthesis*. In this paper these terms are used in a functionally definitive sense as follows:

Analysis: The process of dividing or resolving complex data into constituent elements for the purpose of distinguishing component parts, both separately and with relation to the whole. In application, the method assumes that all significant and relevant information will be collected, recorded, and analyzed.

Synthesis: The combining or integrating of factors of evidence to form a complex unit. In employee selection the process is one of reconstruction of data to identify or particularize the individual as a total personality differing in some respects from all others under consideration.

Clinical method: Intensive study of the individual as a "case" in which both precise psychological techniques and professional judgment are used in collecting, analyzing, comparing, interrelating, and

---

[5] For evidence of this contention see the report of *Proceedings of the Inter-Professions Conference on Education for Professional Responsibility,* New York: Carnegie Press, 1948.

evaluating evidence for the purpose of predicting probable adjustment or response in current and projected situations. In the fullest sense the clinical method presumes diagnosis, prognosis, and treatment to effect desired readjustment. However, in applying the method to employee selection the primary problem is one of predicting response expectancy or probable adjustment in one or more existing or anticipated situations in which performance requirements can be specified.

It was stated in the introductory section of this paper that the philosophy of the psychologist influences his approach to the application of psychology in employee selection. It is inevitable that this will be true. Implicitly, if not explicitly, the applied psychologist superimposes his professional practice upon fundamental theoretical assumptions. The basic assumptions of many of the earlier applied psychologists were restrictive, which in part may account for the barrenness of results obtained through application of psychology to practical problems. The modern psychologist may avoid these restrictions, as does the physician, by basing his practice on a theoretical foundation of rational eclecticism.[6] If this position is accepted then it becomes possible to state the basic theoretical assumptions of the clinical approach to employee selection in relatively simple terms as follows:

1. A *situation* provides *opportunity* for *response*.

2. Depending on facilitating or restricting factors which are characteristics of the individual presented with an opportunity to respond, the situation can be controlled to elicit a predetermined response.

3. The limiting factors of most significance to the psychologist in

---

[6] For a summary of the history of psychological theory and a brief statement of the philosophical bases of psychology see J. F. Brown, "Systematic psychology" in *The Encyclopedia of Psychology*. Philip Lawrence Harriman, (Ed.): New York: The Philosophical Library, Inc., 1946, pp. 885–890. Also compare C. O. Weber, "The concept of scientific law in psychology," *ibid.*, pp. 871–874.

employee selection are individual motivation and capacity for adaptation.[7]

The fundamental principle upon which the clinical method in employee selection must be developed is the principle of individual differences. In determining these differences, the psychologist can, with available tools and techniques, obtain objective evidence on a large variety of individual capacities, but through use of psychological measuring devices alone he can obtain only superficial evidence of motivation.[8] Consequently, evidence obtained through relatively precise measuring instruments is usually insufficient in itself to serve as a basis for professional judgment, particularly in appraising the applicant as a unified personality. Therefore, the psychologist must search for supplementary "clue" evidence, which can only be evaluated through comparison and inference applied within the framework of professional knowledge and common sense.

In using the clinical method the psychologist analyzes all varieties of evidence, whether precise or approximate, quantitative or qualitative, and correlates or synthesizes his observations into a "personal-potential pattern" or "abstract" of the individual being appraised. Weighing this pattern or abstract of the subject or "case," the psychologist engages in diagnosis, utilizing professional knowledge and skill, and formulates a prediction or prognosis most appropriately conceived in terms of actuarial applications of probability to performance expectancy. To be of value to the employer, the prediction must have a probability greater than chance. Furthermore, it must exceed in accuracy (as measured by the theory of limits and probability) other predictions obtainable by simpler (or

---

[7] The application of factors of motivation and capacity in the appraisal of candidates for employment is discussed in Cleeton, *op. cit.,* pp. 15–127.

[8] Cf. Walter V. Bingham, *Aptitudes and Aptitude Testing.* New York: Harper & Brothers, 1937; Mathilda E. Steiner, *The Psychologist in Industry.* Springfield, Ill.: Charles C. Thomas, 1949; and Moore and Hartmann, *op. cit.*

less expensive) methods available to the employer for use in evaluating candidates for employment.

Naturally, in determining suitability of an individual for a given job, or in deciding appropriate placement for the person in one of several jobs, the psychologist applies tests and other psychological measuring devices, but he uses these primarily as one means of obtaining evidence to be considered in assessing the qualities of the candidate and formulating an abstract by which to scale and classify the applicant. He also uses evidence obtained through traditional employment devices, even though such information is less reliable than evidence obtained through the administration of standardized psychological measures. In evaluating evidence allowance must be made for the limited "measured" validity of data obtained through the use of traditional employment devices; and, obviously, any improvements or refinements which may be made in these devices to increase the objectivity of their evidence increases the possibilities of accuracy in professional judgment. However, evidence having limited "measured" validity is often useful because of its "hidden" validity in providing leads for further investigation and exploration, particularly when used as the basis for an evaluative interview or conference with the candidate for employment.

Three elements distinguish the clinical method from the psychometric approach to employee selection:

1. The focus of study is the applicant as a unified personality rather than charts, psychographs, or tabulations of test scores.

2. Professional skill in weighing a wide variety of data is applied in determining the meaning or significance of each item of evidence with reference to the particular personality under review.

3. Diagnostic and prognostic judgments become the basis of selection rather than a statistically derived matrix.[9]

---

[9] Cf. Robert I. Watson, "Diagnosis as an aspect of the clinical method: A review" and William A. Hunt, "The future of diagnostic testing in clinical psychology" in *Readings in the Clinical Method in Psychology*, Robert I. Watson (Ed.): New York: Harper & Brothers, 1949, pp. 395–443.

Selection through the use of psychological tests or other methods of appraisal of individuals who possess the skills and capacities which are prime requisites for the performance of a given job is sound procedure. But to assume that the possession of such skills and capacities alone will make a satisfactory employee is not a logically sound correlate, because each person employed brings to his job a whole personality, which is a unification of numerous and varied interacting characteristics. Only a limited number of these characteristics receive appropriate consideration when employees are chosen primarily on the basis of a matrix constructed by fitting together test scores and other data which are reducible to numerical terms.

The psychometric approach to selection is inadequate from a total-personality-evaluation point of view in that undue emphasis is placed on quantitative standards. This is especially true when these standards are used for the purpose of screening out all applicants except those who meet a successive series of normative requirements. Standards are essential in any employment procedure, but the rigid application of selection standards which permits no exercise of professional judgment results in the removal from further consideration of a disproportionately high number of otherwise promising candidates. From a social point of view the use of a battery of tests as a screening device in employee selection could create difficult problems of occupational adjustment on a broad scale. Hiring according to rigid psychometric specifications without reference to auxiliary information, which is an essential part of the case history of the applicant, greatly increases the number of rejections. Therefore, if any considerable number of business firms in a community were to make use of test scores as the yardstick of employability, a socially unacceptable number of persons would be refused employment; or, more likely, the procedure would break down of its own limitations as it has in some companies where the technique of battery screening has been tried.[10]

---

[10] This problem is treated by the author in greater detail in "Implications of

On a national scale the social implication of arbitrary application of selection standards was demonstrated during the summer and fall of 1950 in the screening of men referred by Selective Service Boards to the examining centers of the Armed Forces. Over a period of three months 60 out of every 100 men examined in the 18–25 age group were rejected as unsuitable for military service. This obviously indefensible rate of rejections caused the Director of Selective Service to suggest that examiners revise their procedures and "look at a man as a complete unit and not try to winnow out the individual who fails to screen through a series of sieves of varying size and form." [11] This suggestion is in accord with the philosophy and practices of clinical psychology because the screening of applicants for employment "through a series of sieves of varying size and form" places emphasis on rejection rather than selection. In the application of the clinical method the approach is reversed: measuring devices are used for the purpose of selecting the most suitable candidates available rather than for the purpose of disqualifying applicants. This is a significant difference because the philosophy implied is positive rather than negative.

In the clinical selection of employees, preliminary details for the preparation of a case history of the applicant are assembled and recorded. The psychologist then seeks not only to determine through the most precise means available the capacity of the applicant to perform the duties of the job but also attempts to determine the adjustment potential of each individual by searching for less precise evidence of motivation and adaptation. Finally, through direct questioning and sometimes through nondirective interviewing, the psychologist tries to penetrate the curtain of reticence and precaution, behind which many applicants retire, in order to obtain evidence relating to emotional stability and individualized modes of

industrial selection by tests" in *Studies in the Psychology of Vocational Adjustment.* Pittsburgh: Carnegie Institute of Technology, 1940, pp. 11–14.

[11] *Barron's Weekly,* October 9, 1950.

behavior which may affect person-to-person relationships in the work environment. In a sense, data with reference to each applicant are appraised both experimentally and experientially.[12] In most employment situations this can be done most conveniently in the three following steps in processing the applicant:

1. The introductory or qualifying stage.
2. The examining stage.
3. The evaluation stage.

In the introductory or qualifying stage, the principal objective is to accumulate information about the applicant which can be used to determine whether he is worthy of further consideration. Rejection occurs only in those cases which fail to meet minimum standards established only for "cut-off" purposes. This results in the retention for further examination of all applicants except those obviously unable to qualify within broad selection limits. In this stage, the sources of information used in qualifying the applicant for the next stage are his personal history and record, statements obtained from former employers, report of the medical examiner, and past social behavior as revealed by confidential sources such as police and credit reports and field investigations. Screening does little harm at this stage if the limits within which applicants are accepted for further review and examination are flexible enough to permit judgment to be used in applying them. The mesh of the screen should be sufficiently coarse to permit the retention of candidates who conceivably might make up in other respects for apparent limitations which may be brought to light in either the qualifying or testing stages.

It is entirely appropriate, in fact imperative, that the psychologist attempt to refine the instruments used for acquiring information to

---

[12] The steps involved in case studies are outlined in John G. Darley, "The structure of the systematic case study in individual diagnosis and counseling," *Readings in the Clinical Method in Psychology, op. cit.,* pp. 209–216. Although this summary of case study procedure is intended for use in counseling students, many of the suggestions offered can be applied in employee selection.

be considered in the introductory or qualifying stage because most application forms, reference rating scales, and experience records in common use could be greatly improved in form and content, to gain in objectivity and thus provide data of higher reliability and validity. Many of these devices could also be changed in style to permit easier recording and utilization of information. However, to assume that these nonstandardized sources of information are either useless or misleading and that they should therefore be disregarded has been demonstrated through practice to be fallacious because important evidence about an applicant is often acquired through sources that do not yield to standardized examining techniques. For example, a telephone conversation with a former employer may reveal crucial information about a particular applicant that could rarely be obtained through the administration of several batteries of tests.

In the qualifying stage, no likely source of information about the applicant should be ignored in reaching a decision either to disqualify the candidate or to proceed further to the next stage of the employment procedure. Here as elsewhere in the clinical method attention should repeatedly be directed toward such questions as: What has the person done in varying circumstances in the past? How has he responded to controlled or relatively well-defined situations? What is revealed by his responses in his relations with other persons in previous work or educational situations? How has the applicant impressed other persons who have observed his responses? Throughout the qualifying stage it is essential that professional judgment be used in determining the probable reliability and predictive significance of evidence obtained. But prejudgment of the fitness of the applicant at this stage should be avoided. The crucial question to be answered is: Does the candidate display sufficient promise to warrant further consideration?

It has been stated in an introductory section of this paper that in early attempts to apply psychology in the selection of employees, many naive assumptions were made in specifying the characteristics and requirements of the jobs for which suitable candidates were being sought. While this is true to a considerable extent today, methods of job analysis and specification are available for use in providing more adequate job descriptions and determining job requirements. Unfortunately, the difficulty of the problem of translating job requirements into terms of human traits and capacities is not always fully recognized and at present the translation is far from complete in most business organizations.

While the most promising research directed toward the determination of the human qualities necessary for various types of work performance has involved the utilization of psychological tests, much research remains to be done if even an approximation to measurement of the wide variety of human elements in job performance is to be achieved. Unfortunately, a considerable amount of the research on employment testing reported in recent years represents little more than repetition of older experimental studies. Until new designs for experimentation in test development for employee selection are created and utilized, the clinical use of tests in employee selection will probably continue to be the most productive utilization of existing instruments of measurement.

Since courses in psychometrics are usually included in the professional training of practically all psychologists they normally feel more at home in the second, or examining, stage of the clinical approach to employment. In that stage the psychologist may even wish to administer all tests himself in order to insure that they are given in just the right manner or to observe the applicant while he is being tested. However, from a professional point of view tests should be considered only as instruments of measurement. The psychologist's chief function is not that of administering tests, but rather that of: (1) determining the kinds of tests which will reveal the information needed to classify the candidate with reference to capacities involved in performing the duties of the job or jobs under consideration; (2) making professionally sound interpretations of the test results; (3) relating these interpretations to information previously obtained; and (4) summarizing evidence and interpretations for further reference in connection with the third or evaluation stage.

Test scores do not provide a *substitute* for other information normally used in employment; however, they do provide a *supplement* to such information. Used as a substitute for other employment information, test scores are likely to be wholly inadequate as a basis for forming judgments about the suitability of prospective employees. This is true because tests usually reveal little more than information on one or more special capacities and personal characteristics which the employee is expected to bring to his job. Thus, if test scores alone are used, important qualities or limitations of the candidate are likely to be overlooked.

Persons not thoroughly familiar with job requirements are likely to conclude that in applying test results it can be assumed that the more capacity an individual displays with reference to a particular job the better the adjustment to be expected. This is not a safe assumption to use in predicting ultimate work adjustment because it has been demonstrated repeatedly that there are broad limits of capacity and skill within which an individual may perform satisfactorily. In fact, an individual who has only acceptable skills and capacities for a given job may meet the requirements of the job more satisfactorily than a person with a higher degree of the same skills and capacities because of other characteristics which contribute to effective work adjustment.

In general it may be said that tests are devices for obtaining samples of behavior under relatively controlled conditions. To the extent that such samples of behavior are related to subsequent behavior on the job, predictions of probable success or failure can be made. Such predictions rarely exceed in accuracy a correlation of .50 with single or multiple criteria for two reasons: (1) no tests have been devised which are perfect instruments of measurement; and (2) factors in personal make-up, not related to the characteristics measured by tests, may make success possible or cause unsatisfactory performance on the job despite the strength or weakness of the characteristics measured by the test. Because of their limitations, sound use of tests in employment requires that scores be related to information obtained from other sources. On the other hand, because of their known reliability and validity, test scores are especially helpful when used as bench marks or points of reference in searching for and interpreting other information.

Determination of the merit of a test, when injected into an employment situation, is found in the answer to the question of how much improvement in selection occurs as a result of its introduction. Is a better qualified employee secured than has previously been hired? Is he easier to train? Does he stay on the job longer? Does he have fewer and less costly accidents? Can he be upgraded? In answering these and similar criterion questions new employees should not only be compared with those who have remained with the company but also with those discharged or who have by their own choice left the job.

The purpose in applying tests is not to attain perfection in selection, but to obtain the highest possible proportion of satisfactory placements among available candidates. Tests aid not only in accomplishing this objective, but also in determining potentiality for ultimate advancement to other work. Accumulation of data on test scores of all persons examined, whether selected or rejected, provides information for determining the type of applicants being attracted. Through continuing studies, ratios can be prepared which will indicate the proportion of those employed at different score levels who will qualify for the job through training or trial on the job as against those who are less likely to survive a probationary or training period. Thus, even though test scores will not always indicate precisely the persons who will prove satisfactory, successive areas of the range within which scores of applicants fall may be used as a basis for predicting the proportion of applicants at each level that will probably prove satisfactory. This permits estimates to be made of the degree to which overemployment will be necessary to fill employment quotas in jobs for which several persons are needed for identical or closely related work activities. By cumulative analysis and interpretation on an actuarial basis of data on test scores versus work performance, it ultimately becomes possible to adjust the cut-off score level or hiring range to the general quality of the available supply of applicants in a fluctuating labor market.

Some employment programs in common use include only those procedures designated in this paper as phases of the qualifying and examining stages. However, if a decision to hire or reject is made at either of these points in the investigation of individual applicants, appraisal is likely to be incomplete because the elements of motivation and personal adjustment potential cannot be judged adequately on the basis of information made available through techniques applied in the qualifying and testing stages. Consequently, assessment of the employment risk involved in hiring an applicant requires that an attempt be made to determine the extent to which he both *can* and *will* adapt his capacities to the job and the particular work environment to which he must respond. This can be accomplished most effectively in a third employment stage, which may be designated as the evaluation stage.

The objective of the evaluation stage is to make an individual selection from a group of candidates who have satisfactorily met standards applied within broad limits in the qualifying and examining stages. In the evaluation stage emphasis is placed on individual characteristics, inasmuch as those individual differences which distinguish the better man from the good man are taken into account. Effort is directed toward the construction from all types of evidence of a well-rounded "picture" or abstract of each applicant, giving appropriate consideration to the extent to which each piece of information or evidence supplements, verifies, or contradicts other evidence. In arriving at this construct, due allowance must be made for subjective factors, in relation both to the applicant and to the sources of information. Furthermore, the person doing the evaluation must guard against personal bias on his own part.

It is in the evaluation stage that the true merit of the psychologist becomes evident. It is here that he becomes a professional practitioner, because not only must each qualification be weighed against other qualifications, but an estimate must be made of the manner in which these qualities—capacities, motivating forces, and elements of personal adjustment—will synthesize or blend together in job performance. Each applicant must be viewed as an individual against a background of employment and job performance standards and must also be rated with reference to probable interaction within the group of which he will become a member in carrying on the work of the job for which he is being considered. In both respects he must be compared with other applicants who are available as well as those persons who have filled the job in the past and those presently engaged in it.

In this and other stages of the clinical method the guiding principle should be that of searching for promising candidates for employment rather than seeking persons whose test profiles match a polyglot scaling device mechanically assembled by fitting together a disjunctive series of statistically calipered psychological "go-no-go" gauges. Operating within the limitations of psychological instruments of measurement now available, the adjunctive elements of evaluation can only be supplied by professional interpretation and inference based on implications as well as data, both qualified and unqualified. In crude parabolic terms it might be observed that, in the clinical method, consideration is often given to the possibility that the shadow cast by an individual may be as important as the physically measurable mass that permits the shadow to occur.

To insure sound professional judgment, the psychologist should establish a means for summarizing and weighing evidence for the purpose of making a professional evaluation of prospective employees. Whether he uses tables, charts, profile graphs, or other implements of the trade is incidental to his ability to weigh and evaluate qualifications and to estimate the potential value of the prospective employee to the business firm. But true professional judgment is possible only when previously accumulated evidence is tested and extended through personal acquaintance with the applicant. To provide opportunity for establishing this acquaintanceship, the third stage of the clinical procedure in employment should include an evaluative interview.

The interview has been widely discussed in psychological circles. It has been ridiculed and condemned and has been challenged as being subjective and unreliable. Yet it continues to be an important instrument in several forms of psychological practice. In applying the clinical method to employee selection painstaking interviewing is indispensable. The interview not only provides an opportunity for reviewing, extending, and collating evidence but, appropriately used, it serves as a means of evaluating, rating, and classifying the applicant from the standpoint of basic premises of job requirements and professional inference.[13]

The evaluative interview calls for the highest order of professional skill. Prior to the interview all previously acquired evidence about the candidate should be summarized and interpreted with reference to such standards as have been established. A preliminary rating of the applicant should also be made on the qualities being sought. With these appraisals in mind the interview should be conducted in a manner which will make possible further appraisal of the

---

[13] The Carnegie group emphasized the importance of the interview in employment procedures. See Walter V. Bingham and Bruce V. Moore, *How to Interview.* New York: Harper & Brothers, 1931. Not only did the authors of this book anticipate current uses of the interview in several areas of psychological practice, but most of the material contained in the book is still sound and applicable. Especially helpful is the chapter on "Learning how to interview," pp. 40–55.

individual characteristics of the applicant and final formulation of an over-all evaluation through judgment of the abstract of the candidate constructed in the mind of the psychologist as the interview progresses. Upon completion of the interview the findings should again be reviewed and a decision reached as to the suitability of the candidate for the employment opportunity under consideration.

The evaluative interview should be a drawing-out or probing process which will elicit sufficient information from the applicant to permit professional inference, make possible the substantiation or revision of previous appraisals, and bring to light new evidence. This can be accomplished if the qualities to be evaluated have been determined in advance and if a series of questions is used which will elicit statements by the applicant that reveal aspects of those qualities. Probably the most productive interview is one that is structured or patterned to permit direct interrogation of the applicant by means of questions formulated in advance. These questions may be arranged in series to permit the interviewer to approach the discussion of a point at issue from different angles. However, the plan of questioning should be sufficiently flexible to permit the interviewer either to probe deeper and deeper into a given topic or to break off the discussion and switch to another topic at any time he feels he has obtained adequate information or has formed impressions which will permit valid inferences to be made.[14]

The interviewer should be on the alert to uncover clue evidence.

---

[14] For examples of the planned interview see:

Richard A. Fear and Byron Jordan, *Employee Evaluation Manual for Interviewers.* New York: Psychological Corporation, 1943.

Robert N. McMurry, *Patterned Interview for Gas Appliance Salesmen.* Servel, Inc., 1944.

E. F. Wonderlic, *Diagnostic Interviewer's Guide.* Privately printed, 1937.

Robert F. Royster, Glen U. Cleeton, and Merwyn A. Kraft, *The Placement Interview for Transit Employees.* American Transit Association, 1946.

Stephen W. Carter and Merwyn A. Kraft, *The Case Interview Plan for Administration of Discipline.* American Transit Association, 1949.

When such evidence is sensed the interviewer may depart from the pattern of previously arranged questions to probe for information that might otherwise be lost by rigid adherence to a predetermined pattern. Some proponents of nondirective interviewing have suggested that this more informal approach be used for the employment interview in somewhat the same manner as the technique is used in employee counseling and psychotherapy. Given about twice the time normally available for employment interviewing and opportunity for several conferences with the candidate, the technique might be used, but its merit as an employment device has as yet not been demonstrated. Inasmuch as the conditions of employment interviewing favor the use of the planned interview in the final or evaluation stage in appraising applicants, its continued use in preference to the nondirective interview seems assured.[15]

It is apparent that to be qualified to render competent judgments in the use of the clinical method in employee selection, the psychologist must have training and experience which goes beyond the limits of academic programs of instruction usually prescribed for graduate students in psychology. In addition to the fundamentals of systematic psychology, preparation can, of course, be achieved to some extent through the study of such subjects as statistics, tests and measurements, guidance and counseling, diagnostic interviewing, survey courses in industrial and clinical psychology, and thorough grounding in the organization and administration of research. Through training, experience, or selective reading the employment psychologist should extend the scope of his field of intellectual familiarity to include labor relations, economics, production methods, operation analysis, work simplification, and job evaluation. In-

---

[15] For discussions of the non-directive interview see:

N. A. Moyer, "Non-directive employment interviewing." *Personnel,* 1948, 24:377–396.

Carl R. Rogers, *Counseling and Psychotherapy.* Boston: Houghton-Mifflin, 1942.

William U. Snyder, *Casebook of Non-directive Counseling.* Boston: Houghton-Mifflin, 1947.

dustrial experience is an asset but not a prime requisite. Also an asset is an understanding of the broad principles of operating and administrative behavior in the work environment, particularly the dynamics of interpersonal and intergroup forces inherent in the business firm as a social organism.[16]

It may be contended that the clinical method of employee selection is too elaborate, and therefore too costly; or that it places too great emphasis on professional judgments which can be rendered only by a competent psychologist.[17] It is difficult to set up a balance sheet to demonstrate either the cost or the value of any type of employment procedure but it is undoubtedly true that oversimplified or makeshift employment routines are the most expensive in the long run. Only the officials of a busniess firm who determine policy are in a position to pass judgment on questions of this type, but it is reasonable to suppose that any procedure of equal merit would cost as much as the procedure herein outlined. In employment for some jobs it may be found that it is either not necessary or not possible to use the clinical method in its entirety. For a given company the point at which minimal returns will be encountered in the application of the method can only be determined by trial and comparison with other procedures. Even though it is found that the clinical method need not or cannot be applied fully over the entire range of employment, the psychologist should be competent to implement the method to the extent warranted by the results obtained at different responsibility and job complexity levels.

As for engaging the services of a psychologist, it may be assumed that if the number of employees in a company is large enough to

---

[16] Cf. Burleigh B. Gardner and David G. Moore, *Human Relations in Industry* (Revised Edition). Richard D. Irwin, 1950.

[17] The clinical approach to employee selection may be used with reasonable effectiveness even though the psychologist serves only in an advisory capacity. For example, see a report of the experience of the Toronto Transportation Commission— W. H. C. Seeley and Merwyn A. Kraft, "Selecting transit operators." *Management Record*, 1948, *10*: 191–193.

justify the maintenance of a centralized personnel department the added expense of employing a full-time staff psychologist can probably be justified.[18] Even in companies which do not require a centralized personnel department, expenditures for the services of a psychologist on a consulting or advisory basis can often be recovered. In a business organization, the added cost of any method for handling human relations which results in the assembling of a competent group of employees who will work together in harmony is always a good investment. Whether this can be accomplished through use of the clinical method in employee relations depends to a considerable degree on the professional competence of the psychologist chosen for the important responsibility of applying it. Here, as in every other professional field, the psychologist must prove his individual merit.[19]

The contribution that can be made by the psychologist in choosing and developing employees is being demonstrated in a constantly increasing number of business firms. This trend toward more extensive use of professional services of psychologists in business and industry is a tribute to the foresight of Dr. Walter V. Bingham, who was among the first to perceive the possibilities of applying psychology in this particular field of human relations. Further tribute to Dr. Bingham is to be found in the fact that many of the procedures and practices still widely used by applied psychologists originated with the Carnegie group under his guidance and sympathetic encouragement. Without the fundamental concepts, practices, and procedures developed by the Carnegie group, the professional use of the clinical method in employee selection as herein outlined would probably not be even remotely possible.

---

[18] The activities of the psychologist need not be, indeed should not be, confined to employee selection. See Steiner, *op. cit.*

[19] "We should consider the individual clinician as a clinical instrument, and study and evaluate his performance exactly as we study and evaluate a test." William A. Hunt, "The future of diagnostic testing in clinical psychology" in *Readings in the Clinical Method in Psychology, op. cit.,* p. 404.

REFERENCES

BINGHAM, W. V.: "On the possibility of an applied psychology." *Psychological Review,* 1923, *30:* 289–305.

The point of view expressed in the following quotation from this article, although published more than a quarter of a century ago, is still sound: "As engineering is to physics, as scientific agriculture is to biology, as medicine is to physiology, as pharmacology is to physiological chemistry, as forestry is to botany, as statistics is to mathematics, as navigation is to astronomy, so ought psychotechnology to be related to psychology."

BINGHAM, W. V.: *Aptitudes and Aptitude Testing.* New York: Harper & Brothers, 1937.

An excellent source of information on tests and their significance for vocational guidance and employee selection.

BINGHAM, W. V., and FREYD, M.: *Procedures in Employment Psychology.* New York: McGraw-Hill, 1926.

Many of the procedures described in this book are still applicable in employment psychology.

BINGHAM, W. V., and MOORE, B. V.: *How to Interview.* New York: Harper & Brothers, 1931.

From its date of publication this book has been and continues to be the basic standard reference on interviewing. Deals with the interview in employment, industrial relations, market studies, commercial surveys, social case work, education, mental clinics, journalism, and as legal evidence. Comprehensive bibliography of literature on the interview to date of publication.

CANTER, R. R.: "Psychologists in industry." *Personnel Psychology,* 1948, *1:* 145–161.

Summary of information relating to the activities of 93 psychologists in business and industry, obtained through a survey made in 1947. Especially significant is an interpretation of professional responsibilities and work functions of the psychologist in industry.

CARTER, S. W., and KRAFT, M. A.: *The Case Interview Plan for Administration of Discipline.* New York: American Transit Association, 1949.

In language for the layman describes the clinical approach to a special problem of supervision.

CLEETON, G. U.: "Implications of industrial selection by tests." In *Studies in the Psychology of Vocational Adjustment*. Pittsburgh: Carnegie Institute of Technology, 1940.

The problem of social limitations of employee selection by tests is explored.

CLEETON, G. U.: *Making Work Human*. Antioch Press, 1949.

Deals with responsibilities of management with respect to both the economic and psychological aspects of human relations problems in industry. Contains a chapter on "Research and Judgment in Work Relations."

FEAR, R. A., and JORDAN, B.: *Employee Evaluation Manual for Interviewers*. New York: Psychological Corporation, 1943.

Suggests procedures for evaluative interviewing.

GARDNER, B. B., and MOORE, D. G.: *Human Relations in Industry* (Revised Edition). Richard D. Irwin, 1950.

The thesis of the business firm as a social institution is presented with illustrative instances.

GOOD, I. J.: *Probability and the Weighing of Evidence*. New York: Hafner Publishing Company, 1950.

A mathematical approach.

HARRIMAN, P. L. (Ed.): *The Encyclopedia of Psychology*. New York: The Philosophical Library, Inc., 1946.

Contains brief summaries of the history and principles of systematic psychology; an attempt is made to classify and compare conflicting concepts of modern psychology.

Manual of Employment Interviewing. Research Report No. 9. New York: American Management Association, 1946.

Contains bibliography of selected references on the interview.

McMURRY, R. N.: *Patterned Interview for Gas Appliance Salesmen*. Evansville, Indiana: Servel, Inc., 1944.

An example of a fully structured interview, in which the questions to be asked are stated and accompanying each question is an indication of the personality characteristic to be evaluated by the interviewer on the basis of the interviewee's responses.

MOORE, B. V., and HARTMANN, G. W.: *Readings in Industrial Psychology*. New York: Appleton-Century-Croft, Inc., 1931.

Selections on traditional employment devices, tests, and the interview are included; also contains good material on selection procedures, placement, guidance, motivation, and individual and social adjustment.

MOYER, N. A.: "Non-directive employment interviewing." *Personnel,* 1948, *24:* 377–396.

A report of use of non-directive interviewing in employee selection.

ORDWAY, S. H., JR., and O'BRIEN, J. C.: *An Approach to More Objective Tests*. Society for Personnel Administration, Pamphlet No. 2. Washington, D. C.; June, 1939.

Contains a discussion of panel interviewing.

The Placement Interview. Civilian Personnel Pamphlet No. 15, War Department, 1945.

Classification of applicants through use of the patterned interview is discussed.

Proceedings of the Inter-Professions Conference on Education for Professional Responsibility. New York: Carnegie Press, 1948.

A series of papers in which respective approaches to professional education for medicine, law, business administration, engineering, and the ministry are presented. Common methods of thought are explored with reference to the objectives of professional education, the content and method of professional instruction, and humanistic and social education as preparation for professional responsibility and citizenship.

"Psychologists in business." *Forbes Magazine,* Aug. 1, 1950, *66:* 12–13.

An interpretation for business managers of psychological services, particularly as rendered by consulting organizations.

ROETHLISBERGER, F. J., and DICKSON, W. J.: *Management and the Worker*. Cambridge: Harvard University Press, 1942.

Analysis of employee morale on the basis of attitude surveys and non-directive interviewing in employee counseling. Contains illustrative material based primarily on experiments conducted at the Hawthorne plant of the Western Electric Company.

ROGERS, C. R.: *Counseling and Psychotherapy*. Boston: Houghton-Mifflin, 1942.

Non-directive interviewing in counseling and therapy.

ROSENZWEIG, S. (with Kate L. Kogan): *Psychodiagnosis.* New York: Grune and Stratton, 1949.

Presents the interpretative use of tests in contrast to their normative psychometric application in clinical diagnosis. Includes illustrative case material.

ROYSTER, R. F., CLEETON, G. U., and KRAFT, M. A.: *The Placement Interview for Transit Employees.* New York: American Transit Association, 1946.

Description of a planned interview, sample interview questions, and suggestions for effective interviewing.

SEELEY, W. H. C., and KRAFT, M. A.: "Selecting transit operators." *Management Record,* 1948, *10:* 191–193.

A report of the use of the clinical method in employee selection by the Toronto Transportation Commission.

SHAFFER, L. F.: *The Psychology of Adjustment.* Boston: Houghton-Mifflin, 1936.

A systematic discussion of motivating factors in their relation to individual adjustment. Contains a brief discussion of the use of direct and indirect evidence in case studies.

SNYDER, W. U.: *Casebook of Non-directive Counseling.* Boston: Houghton-Mifflin, 1947.

Illustrative material in use of non-directive techniques.

STEINER, MATHILDA E.: *The Psychologist in Industry.* Springfield, Ill.: Charles C. Thomas, 1949.

Contains an outline of industrial applications of psychology, a list of tests and techniques used in employee selection and placement, and a comprehensive bibliography on selection, placement, observing the worker on the job, and counseling the worker.

TARBELL, A. W.: *The Story of Carnegie Tech, 1900 to 1935.* New York: Carnegie Press, 1937.

Contains a brief historical statement on the formation of the Division of Applied Psychology at Carnegie Institute of Technology, including evidence that Carnegie was the first institution to establish a chair of applied psychology.

UHRBROCK, R. S.: "The personnel interview." *Personnel Psychology,* 1948, *1:* 273–302.

A survey of interview practices with emphasis on the need for research.

WATSON, R. I., (Ed.): *Readings in the Clinical Method in Psychology.* New York: Harper & Brothers, 1949.

An excellent survey of recent literature on the clinical method as applied in counseling and therapy in schools, hospitals, and clinics.

WONDERLIC, E. F.: *Diagnostic Interviewer's Guide.* Privately printed, 1937.

Four pages of questions for interviewing with a suggested scheme for rating responses.

11

A National Scholarship Program: Methods, Problems, Results

John M. Stalnaker

Director of Studies
Association of American Medical Colleges

In November, 1944, Walter S. Mack, Jr., then president of Pepsi-Cola Company, approached the writer for help in developing a national scholarship program of wider coverage and more generous terms than any of the existing or earlier private scholarship programs. Mr. Mack had been considering the idea for some time; he had consulted several educators and had investigated other programs. He was now ready to act.

The broad general plans for the scholarships had at that time been roughly outlined. Mr. Mack sought help in modifying the plans into a workable program and in executing the program. After study, the writer proposed in some detail how such a program could be developed with the necessary safeguards and operated for the benefit of the schools and the youth of the country. This paper is a description of how the program was developed, the basis for the regulations, the general outcomes, and an evaluation of the venture which, when completed in 1952, will have cost approximately two million dollars.

CONTROL AND CONDITIONS

The entire program was to be under the complete control, both as to policy and operation, of a separate corporation which should consist of educators. Accordingly, the Pepsi-Cola Scholarship Board was incorporated in New Jersey on February 1, 1945. The original Board members included distinguished educators: Floyd W. Reeves, president, Herman L. Donovan, Milton S. Eisenhower, Paul E. Elicker, Alvin C. Eurich, Henry T. Heald, Mordecai W. Johnson, Walter S. Mack, Jr., Marjorie H. Nicolson, Paul A. Rehmus, and John M. Stalnaker. At a later date the Board was enlarged to include the following group: Francis L. Bacon, Edmund E. Day, Harold W. Dodds, Rev. Robert Gannon, S.J., Willard E. Goslin, Frank P. Graham, Rufus C. Harris, and Wilbur K. Jordan. John M. Stalnaker was named Director and Secretary-Treasurer of the corporation.

The program was designed for the benefit of the schools and the youth of the country. There was no tie-in with the bottlers or the advertising agency of the Company. At no time was the Scholarship Board or the director of the program asked to alter or adjust the program on any basis other than to make a greater educational contribution. The philosophy underlying the program was that a corporation should be a good member of the community. The sponsoring company doubtless felt that the promotion of a thoroughly worth-while venture, widely approved by the public which consumes soft drinks, will alter the soft drink preferences of that public. This theory has not been adequately tested, but it is not generally supported by the advertising fraternity or by business executives who control expenditures for public relations and advertising.

The members of the Scholarship Board appreciated that there is waste of our most valuable national resource—raw brain power. Numerous studies have shown that many of the most able high school seniors do not go on to college. Any program which encourages able high school students to consider undertaking further training by supporting a few select ones in college is worthy of support. Thus, the Board members gave generously of their support, and in general the program received the help and encouragement of both secondary school and college groups.

RESTRICTIONS

A commercially financed scholarship program must, if it is to succeed, meet a number of requirements, and certain other conditions are desirable although not essential. In setting up the Pepsi-Cola scholarship program, efforts were made to meet the following requirements:

1. First, there was to be no advertising of the program or publicity promoted by the Company. This provision, readily agreed to and scrupulously lived up to by Pepsi-Cola, is more precautionary than essential. Educators are wary of the advertising of any project participated in by the schools, especially when sponsored by a firm whose products may be purchased by the pupils.

2. Participation in the program should not require, request, or even indirectly suggest, that the use of the sponsor's products is necessary for participation. Here again, Pepsi-Cola Company consented. No fees, premiums, or pledges were required of participants or winners.

3. There should be no obligation on the part of the school, the participants, or the winners, other than to succeed in their college work. The sole obligation of the Pepsi-Cola scholar is that he succeed in the field of study of his own selection and in the college

of his choice. Success is determined by the regulations of the college he attends. Honor grades are not required.

4. The program should be designed so that it has no influence on the curriculum. Commercial sources should not attempt even in mild ways to dictate what is taught in the schools. The Pepsi-Cola scholarship program was broad. No course or type of study was urged.

5. No restriction was to be placed on what a winner should study, where he should study, or what career he should train for. Both boys and girls were equally eligible to win. While such complete freedom creates certain difficulties in the selection process, it has many advantages.

6. The program should have a beneficial influence on the schools and the pupils. It was hoped that the scholarship program would encourage sound study habits, direct the attention of the more able pupils to the possibilities of college, and call attention on the part of the advisers to the availability of help for unusual pupils who might not be considering further formal education.

7. The scholarship program was designed so that the time and effort on the part of any school official, administrator, or teacher would be small compared with the benefits of participation to the school and the pupil. In any case, the absolute time required of any one voluntarily helping with the program was small.

8. The school should be informed of the individual results of its pupils on any tests, and the names and schools of all winners. This was done. All procedures were announced and the results were open for inspection by all concerned.

9. The awards should be large enough to be of significant value to the winners, and the number of winners should be large enough to justify national participation. Most commercially sponsored scholarships are small in amount—some pitifully small—and few are offered. The Pepsi-Cola program offered scholarships amounting to over $300,000 annually.

10. The program should be carefully planned and efficiently administered. The general consensus was that the Pepsi-Cola program was well handled from the point of view of the schools, participating pupils, and colleges.

11. No travel should be required of the participants, and no expense on the part of the school.

12. The scholarship program, in both its planning and its administration, should be handled by educators, a requirement met by almost no other commercially sponsored scholarship program.

13. The program should be noncontroversial and avoid political, religious, and other areas where sharp differences of opinion may divide school groups. The implication is not that controversial material has no place in the schools, but rather that it has no place in a commercially financed program in the schools.

14. Awards should be assigned on the basis of the ability of the applicants without regard to sex, race, creed, or any conditions of possible advantage to the sponsor. In the Pepsi-Cola scholarship program, the sponsor had no hand in the selection, or knowledge of the results until they were announced. Modern selection techniques were followed to the letter, with no exceptions.

FIRST SELECTION

At the first meeting of the Pepsi-Cola Scholarship Board on January 31, 1945, the general plans were reviewed and alterations made to make the program conform to the best thought of the Board. The deliberate, mature consideration of the Board resulted in many valuable suggestions, not alone at this stage, but also at every step in the development of the program. Although the war was still in progress and young men were being drafted, the decision was made to initiate the program with the group of high school seniors graduating in May and June of 1945. A provision was made to hold the scholarship of any winner who entered the armed forces. Because of the world conditions, the lateness of getting the program under way, and the general skepticism of the schools toward commercially sponsored programs, it was anticipated that participation would be light.

Announcements sent to the public and parochial four-year secondary schools in the United States on February 20, 1945, stated that 118 scholarships, each for four college years, were being offered. Two scholarships were available for students in each state and the District of Columbia, and twenty additional scholarships restricted to Negroes in the states having a segregated school system for the colored.

Each scholarship consisted of full tuition and required fees for four years to any accredited college or university in the United States, plus $25.00 a month in cash to help defray expenses during the nine school months of each year and a travel allowance of three cents a mile for one trip a year from home to college and return. The winner could go to any college and pursue any course of study leading to the B.A. or B.S. degree. The exact value of the scholarship in dollars depended upon how far the winner travelled to college and what college he selected. In one case it has amounted to $4650; at the other extreme, one scholarship amounted to $1111.

In addition to the scholarships, college entrance prizes were offered to the runners-up. For the first program, these awards were entirely honorary, although each winner's name was listed in a booklet sent to every college in the United States. During the next three programs, the college entrance prize paid $50.00 to the winner provided he entered college. The total cost of these prizes, over $85,000, was believed justified by the educational good accomplished, in spite of the small amount of each award. Many colleges offered other scholarships to these runners-up.

The program was altered slightly in certain regards in each of the following three selection periods, but the basic features remained the same. As improvements became possible, they were instituted. For example, Alaska, Puerto Rico, and Hawaii were included and allowed one scholarship each, the testing procedures were perfected, communications with the schools were improved, etc.

The Pepsi-Cola scholarship program as finally evolved attempted to meet all the requirements already discussed and addressed itself to the selection of potential intellectual leaders. It was recognized that mistakes would be made, and that some compromises were necessary to make the program acceptable to large numbers of schools. The fundamental question was whether or not the schools would support this type of commercially sponsored program.

THE SCHOLARSHIP PROGRAM

Briefly, the program required participation by the school rather than the individual. The school registered for the program. To keep the total participation, and thus the costs, within reason, each school was allowed to be represented by at least two seniors, but by not more than 5 per cent of the senior class. Representatives were chosen by the senior class in election, with such guidance and help as the administrative officers cared to give the seniors. This process, it was hoped, would result in the selection of students with demonstrated characteristics of leadership. It is a sound democratic process of psychological value. While this aspect of the program did not succeed unqualifiedly with all schools and posed special problems, it was a first approach to a neglected area. The elected representatives then took a preliminary test prepared and scored by the Educational Testing Service of Princeton, New Jersey, and administered by the schools. The highest-scoring pupils in each state were then invited to take the College Board test which is administered under supervised conditions, thus protecting the officials of the schools participating in the program. The fees were paid by the scholarship program. The two highest-scoring candidates in each state were awarded the scholarships and the next ten were given entrance prizes. In states having segregated school systems, separate awards were made for Negro pupils. Unless there was financial need, the scholarships were made honorary. The difficulties of determining financial need are many. There are some virtues to the simple approach. In this case, the determination was made on the basis of a simple declaration by the parent.

PARTICIPATION

Schools were invited to participate in the scholarship program, and approval of the program was obtained by the many controlling groups, both national and local. Announcements were placed in school journals and school papers. Letters and information were sent to the entire list of secondary schools.

In the four years the selection program operated, over 14,000 different high schools took part, or over half of all the high schools in the country. A total of 126,471 seniors actually were tested. The detailed figures are given in Table I.

TABLE I. PARTICIPATION IN THE PEPSI-COLA SCHOLARSHIP PROGRAM

Year	Schools Participating	Seniors Examined	Scholarships Awarded	Entrance Prizes
1945	3,741	14,584	121	536
1946	6,647	27,395	122	624
1947	9,182	38,380	124	641
1948	10,629	46,112	122	586
TOTAL	14,776	126,471	489	2,387

From Table I it can be seen that in 1948, the year when the participation was greatest and the program perfected, 10,629 schools entered the program, represented by 46,112 tested seniors. These seniors were elected to take the test by senior classes totaling about 850,000.

Of the 14,776 different schools which participated, 5812 participated in only one of the four years. The first year, in spite of the late start, 3741 schools took part, but 609 of these schools did not enter any of the three subsequent years. In 1946, 6647 schools took part and 1022 did not participate again. Of the 1947 group, 1387 did not again enter. In 1948, the final year, 2794 schools which had not participated before entered the program. Although each year some schools dropped out, the increase of new schools more than made up for them. In the final year, almost three times as many schools took part as in the first year, and 1447 more than in the preceding year.

Had the program continued, the number of schools participating each year would doubtless have reached a ceiling of probably eleven or twelve thousand. Of the 25,218 schools on the mailing list, about 41 per cent were schools of a total student population of less than 100. Many of them do not have seniors every year.

In spite of objections to commercially sponsored programs, this scholarship program gained wide recognition and acceptance by the secondary schools of the country.

AWARDS

During the four years in which selections were made, a total of 489 paying four-year college scholarships were awarded and 27 honorary scholarships (no monetary value because of no serious financial need). Also, 26 paying three-year graduate fellowships were awarded, but this program is not discussed here. In addition, 2387 seniors were awarded college entrance prizes, 1851 of which carried a pledge of $50 provided the winner entered college for academic work within a year. Up to July 1, 1950, 1711 of these awards had been paid. Thus, 92 per cent of the prize winners of the last three selections are known to have entered college.

Table II gives the status of the scholars for each of the four years as of January 1, 1951.

TABLE II. STATUS OF PEPSI-COLA SCHOLARS AS OF JANUARY 1, 1951

Status	Number of Scholars Selected in Each of Four Years								Total
	1945		1946		1947		1948		
	White	Negro	White	Negro	White	Negro	White	Negro	
In college	1	2	3	5	95	13	100	14	233
Graduated *	85	12	85	10	1	—	—	—	193
Relinquished									
Voluntarily	11	2	14	1	2	6	1	1	38
Failure	4	3	—	2	4	2	3	3	21
Held †	1	—	1	1	1	—	—	—	4
TOTAL	102	19	103	19	103	21	104	18	489

* Includes 12 whose scholarships expired prior to graduation because they were taking five-year programs.

† Scholarships are held for students in the armed services and for certain other reasons such as illness.

WHERE THE WINNERS GO TO COLLEGE

In evaluating the success of the scholars in college, one should appreciate how the group was selected and the freedom given the winners. In the first year, for example, in one state the winner from the segregated schools was selected from only 17 participants. She has now graduated from Fisk and has entered the teaching profession. In the general program in the first year, two winners of scholarships from the state of Delaware were selected from only 35 participants. (Both of the winners have now graduated from college and one plans graduate study.) In the same year, the two winners from Pennsylvania were selected from 1198 participants (one of whom dropped out of college at the end of his junior year to marry). In some cases where participation was light, the winners were known to be poor college material. Most of the winners, however, were promising.

The winners were usually given publicity in their own communities, and the flattery resulted in some of the winners of modest ability and training selecting colleges and programs quite beyond their reach. No one was prevented from selecting any program or any college to which he could gain admission, and some colleges assumed all winners were good enough to offset poor preparation. One winner, for example, was admitted by a difficult engineering school normally demanding more preparation than he had had. After one semester he was on probation, and according to regulations his scholarship should have been withdrawn. The attitude of the Board was, however, a generous one. In this case, the scholarship was suspended until he completed one semester satisfactorily, when it was reinstated. Transferring to another type of institution nearer his home, he made a creditable record, graduating in the upper half of his class after a full program of extra-curricular activities.

A winner of very modest endowment from a small southern segregated school could, if admitted, go to a large northern university or college. Failure in some of these cases was inevitable, and indeed New York University, Barnard, and the University of Wisconsin, among others, were the institutions where some of these individuals failed. On the other hand, some of the colored group have graduated from Radcliffe, Columbia, and Northwestern, and others are progressing well at Harvard, Oberlin, Swarthmore, Columbia, Cornell, and Catholic University of America.

The winners picked almost every variety of college and every type of course. As the program grew and the selection therefore became more rigorous, a large proportion of the winners picked the large well-known institutions. In all, however, a total of 191 different colleges and universities were attended by the scholars. The most popular institution was Harvard which a total of some 43 scholars attended. Then, in order of popularity with this group were: Stanford (26), Massachusetts Institute of Technology (23), Yale (19), Howard (15), Chicago (15), Cornell (13), Fisk (12), Notre Dame (11), Princeton (9), and Northwestern (9).

Table III gives the general area of study of the scholars. The subject-matter has ranged from the classics which attracted 4 of the scholars to chemistry which has drawn 49 and physics with 30. The classicists have all been excellent students, 2 having graduated (both Phi Beta Kappa), and 2 being still in college. The science majors include some equally promising students.

TABLE III. AREA OF CONCENTRATION OF PEPSI-COLA SCHOLARS

Area of Concentration	Number of Scholars				
	1945	1946	1947	1948	*Total*
Biological sciences	10	15	8	9	42
Physical sciences	23	25	38	35	121
Social sciences	22	28	24	33	107
Humanities	31	28	22	26	107
Engineering	11	7	14	11	43
Other (business, physical education, agriculture, etc.)	4	1	3	—	8
Not determined	20	18	15	8	61
TOTAL	121	122	124	122	489

The physical sciences have attracted the largest number of this promising group of scholars, with the social sciences and humanities tied for second place in popularity. Engineering has been selected by 43 of these scholars and the biological sciences have come fifth in popularity.

In determining the selection procedures, an effort was made to allow all types to compete on as equal a footing as possible. The wide variety of courses of study chosen indicates success in this regard.

EVALUATION

The success of a scholarship venture as large and broad as this one is difficult if not impossible to determine. What has the influence of the program been? Has it stimulated able high school seniors to give more serious consideration to college possibilities? Has it pointed out to colleges the availability of excellent material in every section of the country? Has it helped an able group to a type of education which would not otherwise have been possible?

Even the success of the winners in their college work is difficult to determine. The freedom of the winners to go to any college and to pursue any type of program of studies, however desirable, introduced so many chance factors that descriptions of what happened seem to be the only "measure." If the Negro from a deplorably feeble segregated school, instead of electing a large northern college, had picked a college in his own region, he now would be listed in the success column. If the lad planning to go to his small state institution, now with the scholarship help elects a more difficult and distant university, where his record is only mediocre, how can one measure the gain to him? Surely, there is something not measured in grade points.

The program made possible a type of education which for many would otherwise have been impossible. "Without this scholarship," writes one winner, "I would now be working on a construction gang along with my father. With it I am going to one of the finest universities in the world, living in a new atmosphere of intellectual freedom and thinking really for the first time in my life. I am preparing for a career in which I can perform useful services. Our society being structured as it is, I would never have had a chance to meet the girl I am going to marry had it not been for the Pepsi-Cola scholarship."

A grateful foreign-born mother writes: "I often wonder how you can visualize the immense happiness you bring to thousands of families." She goes on at some length to tell her story of difficulties overcome to see that her two children are given an education. The Pepsi-Cola scholarship helped to make her dreams come true.

Her son, with the help of the scholarship, graduated *magna cum laude* and now is training for a profession.

The record must be examined even though it does not point to a clear-cut conclusion. The few failures are more interesting in some ways than the many successes, which were anticipated.

On January 1, 1951, approximately 10 per cent of the winners had lost or given up their scholarships. The reasons are many. Of the scholarship winners, 13 per cent (10 of 77) from the segregated schools and 2.6 per cent of the others (11 of 412) had failed for what appear to be scholastic reasons. Five of these had been having psychological difficulties; one is a failure because he would not meet the physical education requirement and was therefore dropped after two years with an otherwise satisfactory record. An unwillingness to conform to rules which are judged unwise is not accepted by colleges.

The 38 who relinquished their scholarships for other reasons than scholastic difficulties almost defy classification. Each one has a unique situation. Even the two suicides differ basically. One scholar died while in the army from unknown causes, bringing the total deaths in this young group to three. One winner did not enter college as required, deciding to stay out for a time, and thus lost her scholarship. Ten of the girls and one boy left college because of marriage, although 18 girls and 8 boys who held scholarships married and continued in college. In fact, 5 of the girls and 2 of the boys continued in college after becoming parents. In at least one of the cases, the college rules demanded that she leave, marriage of students while in college being prohibited. She married a Pepsi-Cola college entrance prize winner attending the same college.

Others relinquished their scholarships to enter Annapolis (where outside help is not needed), to enter training for the priesthood, to go to a school of music, because financial aid was no longer necessary (and the amount paid was refunded to the Board), because of illness in the family, because of mental trouble, etc.

The 412 scholarship winners from the general program and the 77 from the segregated program are reduced by the 21 failures and 38 relinquished to 373 and 57 respectively. The group is further reduced, by the graduation of 181 and the successful completion of four years of a five-year program of 12, to 202 and 35 respectively, or a total of 237 whose scholarships are still active.

Honors won by the group are many. One of the group selected in the first year, 1945, has won a Rhodes scholarship. Two of the girl scholarship winners married men who won Rhodes scholarships. Of the graduates, about one-third have graduated with some scholastic distinction: 39 have been elected to Phi Beta Kappa, 5 to Sigma Xi, and 44 others have won similar distinctions. One winner—a blind boy from Nevada—won the highest honors in the history of his institution. Other types of honors and activities are too numerous to permit description.

One other type of evaluation is possible. What influence did this program have on consumers of soft drinks? The program was designed and operated for the benefit of the country and not to promote the sale of the product of its financial sponsor. Nonetheless such a program is of widespread interest, and the sponsor must gain some recognition in the eyes of the public. If a program as carefully controlled as this one is to gain financial support, it must bring some return to the sponsor in prestige, sales, or in some terms understood by the directors and the stockholders.

To test the influence of the scholarship program, Pepsi-Cola Company was urged by the director of the scholarship program to have an independent established survey firm check on the attitude of the public toward the program. Several dependable firms were suggested. The survey was subsequently made without the knowledge of the Scholarship Board or its director and therefore without any influence of the staff of the scholarship office on the results. The survey was based on interviews of somewhat over 3000 persons, all users of soft drinks. All those interviewed were between the ages of 15 and 29. The sample was believed to be a representative one of all people in the United States within the age group. There were 180 localities, including farming areas, included. The interviewers did not know what firm was sponsoring the survey or its purpose.

Several facts of possible significance emerge from the findings. Exposure to the scholarship program appeared to dispose an appreciable number of people to choose Pepsi-Cola as a drink. The more the people knew about the program, the larger the proportion drinking Pepsi-Cola. Where the persons had participated in the selection of participants, the preference for Pepsi-Cola was high. As an idea, sponsorship of a scholarship program was best liked among a variety of possible activities which a soft drink maker might sponsor, and furthermore the respondents admitted they would be inclined toward the drink of such a sponsor.

The effect of the program, as judged by persons of some experience in the field of advertising and public relations, was greater than anticipated and relative to other approaches, good. Nonetheless, the program must have been judged as too expensive to justify its continuation. The Company decided not to finance additional scholarships after four groups had been selected.

Had the program been continued on the scale it was going, the cost would have been well under half the annual cost of well-known weekly comedy radio programs of half an hour's duration. The radio program attracts a large audience who are then given a commercial. The scholarship program had no specific commercial— one would not have been acceptable to the schools or to the Scholarship Board. Without a commercial, the program has been shown to have had a value to the sponsor. The scholarship program, like popular radio programs, had an audience and a large one. It was planned as a continuing program, and its full effect could not be determined until it had been continued for several more years. Even in four years, however, it had a measurable effect.

EXPENSES

The total cost of the activities of the Pepsi-Cola Scholarship Board cannot be determined until the programs are completed. The general administration of the programs has cost about half a million dollars. This sum covers the costs of circularizing the schools, registration, testing, correspondence, publications, research, etc. Every step was taken with care. Thoroughness rather than economy was the keynote.

For tuition for the scholars about three quarters of a million dollars will be required. Wherever a winner is in another program, such as the Reserve Officers Training Program of the Navy, or receives full tuition from the G.I. Bill, no tuition is paid by the scholarship. The travel allowances, each small in themselves, will total around $67,000. The monthly allowance it is estimated will finally cost over $400,000. The College Entrance Prizes cost $85,500.

The fellowship program which sent some 26 graduates to advanced study will cost somewhat under $100,000.

Thus, the total costs will be of the order of $1,900,000.

GROWING UP

Even a preliminary report such as this one cannot properly be concluded without acknowledging the enjoyment that the director and staff of this program have received from working with such an able and challenging group of promising youngsters. Selected at the high school senior level, from every section of the country, from almost every type of background, this group looked toward almost every type of training, to be received in colleges of every variety. Watching them grow up, learning of their problems, their successes and occasional failures, even their romances, provides a rich experience.

Dealing almost exclusively by correspondence has its limitations. Yet one comes to understand what college has meant to some of these scholars. Many of them had their first experience in a part of the country very different from that in which they had grown up: a student from Hawaii, a Japanese-American girl, attended Swarthmore; students from Arkansas, Nevada, Washington, Texas, and many another state are becoming familiar with New England; students from the middle west and the Atlantic seaboard have seen the far west for the first time; half a dozen students have taken advantage of the "junior year abroad" offered by their colleges to see Scotland, France, or Switzerland, and to learn the culture and customs of another land. Virtually all these experiences would have been impossible for these young people without the financial assistance furnished by their scholarships.

Then, too, the able youngsters from the farm and the small town were able to go away from home for the first time and live in the city. Winners came from such small towns as Florence Villa, Florida; Dallas, Georgia; Sayreton, Alabama; North Cove, North Carolina; Purcelleville, Virginia; Clayton, Delaware; Kemmerer, Wyoming; Oxford, Massachusetts; Eureka, Montana; Spencer, Idaho; Conde, South Dakota; and Dorchester, Nebraska, to name but a few of the smaller towns supplying winners. Of course others came from New York City, Detroit, Philadelphia, Memphis, San Diego, Denver, St. Louis.

The letters from these scholars, few in most cases—for they live busy lives in their academic careers and the Pepsi-Cola Scholarship Board is not very personal to them—reveal something of their thinking. "The world has become broader and deeper," writes a scholar after one year at one of our leading universities, and he goes on to explain why. "I have learned about things I never knew existed before," writes another. "Beginning in the middle of my junior year I have been developing a social consciousness," writes a serious senior. "Here at M.I.T. I am studying chemical engineering and finding it very interesting even if I'm in a hopeless muddle most of the time. I do, however, manage to get to Glee Club rehearsals and meetings of the American Institute of Chemical Engineers," is an expression from a successful winner. A scholar at Harvard says simply, "I plan to make astrophysics the field of my future career," and goes on to outline his plans for analyzing individual stars with the spectograph of a 61-inch reflector.

"It seemed like a miracle when Pepsi made it possible for me to be at the University," is a sentiment frequently expressed. "The more I appreciate this University, the more I realize what an opportunity the Pepsi-Cola scholarship has given me," is the way another winner expresses his appreciation. After a description of her program, a scholar writes, "College is wonderful . . . I want you to know that I'm very happy, very busy, and very grateful to you all for making this education possible."

"I realize that this year might have been impossible if it had not been for the Pepsi-Cola scholarship. I can never thank you enough. Not only does the Board make my college career possible, but also it proves to be an incentive for doing one's best." A Harvard man (whose sister won the scholarship the following year) expresses a thought common to many of the group: "We hope that your investment in the development of our minds and personalities will some day reap dividends. Already it has proved worth while to us, for an enlightened mind knows no boredom."

From the correspondence and records there is a residue which cannot easily be quantified or put into a form which proves anything, and yet it is revealing. It appears to give some evidence that the program did contribute in a significant fashion to the development of many young promising men and women.

The commercial sponsorship of a program of such dimensions took both vision and courage. A much larger corporation has for many years sponsored a symphony radio program (without commercials), and other examples of occasional corporation support of activities of value to the community and the country are not unheard of. Yet for a corporation of the size of Pepsi-Cola Company to undertake a broad-based national scholarship program is remarkable. To Mr. Walter Mack goes credit for making the scholarship program possible. He saw in the program an investment that pays life-long dividends to everyone. Such commercially sponsored scholarships may well be one means of perpetuating democracy and of better integrating the corporation into the life of the country. Teamwork between industry and education can promote new high levels of citizenship.

To Pepsi-Cola Company goes credit for seeing the program through. To the Scholarship Board goes credit for allowing their names and talents to be drawn upon to formulate and promote what is probably the largest private scholarship venture ever undertaken by industry, and, so far as is known, the only one under the complete control, both as to policy and to operation, of a group of educators.